Endorsements for
Training to Reign with God

Having known Marcia for several decades, I continue to be impressed by her ongoing desire to press forward in Christ and to share what she has learned to benefit God's people. She has a deep and abiding love for God as well as a faithful commitment to bring healing, encouragement, and empowerment to her brothers and sisters in Christ. Having been through many grueling times herself, she knows how to come alongside others as a good shepherd who has navigated through deserts and has found the water of life.

– *The Rev. A. Robert Bethancourt*

I have sat under Marcia's mentorship for many years and her ability to teach in practical ways always hits the mark. Through her teaching you will find ways to understand and live out Biblical principles. She uncovers hidden treasure that you missed. You will be forever grateful.

– *Eve Troutt, Grant Writer*

My walk with God has been strengthened over the years by attending Marcia's mentoring classes. I have received deliverances, healings, and a deeper understanding of God's word. Marcia has taught me how to think, speak, pray, and listen more closely to the Holy Spirit.

– *Serena Perez*

I was blessed to participate in the Tuesday Zoom meetings and the noon prayer sessions. Several personal prayer sessions with Marcia brought deliverance from strongholds that were holding me back from the life God has for me. Marcia is a dedicated teacher with whom I have grown spiritually by leaps and bounds. She has faithful dedication and love for her flock.

– Ella Peterson

TRAINING *to* REIGN *with* God

TRAINING *to* REIGN *with* God

THE CHRISTIAN GUIDE TO SPIRITUAL MATURITY

MARCIA CHANG VOGL

Copyright © 2022 by Marcia Chang Vogl

All rights reserved. No part of this book may be reproduced, distributed, or transmitted in any form or by any means, including photocopying, recording, or other electronic or mechanical methods, without the prior written permission of the author, except in the case of brief quotations embodied in critical reviews and certain other noncommercial uses permitted by copyright law.

Published by Hidden With Christ Ministries

ISBN (paperback): 978-1-7354447-2-7
ISBN (ebook): 978-1-7354447-1-0

Book design by Christy Day, Constellation Book Services

Printed in the United States of America

Gratitude

The Lord put it on my heart to write this book to help others walk with Him. I share peeks into my life as He directs and blesses me. I am grateful to my Bethany Projects team who partners with me in ministry and let me be creative to experiment in new moves of the Holy Spirit. We discover new ways to pray, worship, and rejoice. They encourage and celebrate with me.

This book would not be a reality without the help of my coaches, Christina Smith, Sara Brown, and Geoffrey Berwind. My first reader, Linda Graham, and proof reader, Ella Peterson, also invested in this project. I am grateful for them all.

Contents

Foreword		*xi*
Introduction		*1*
Prologue		*7*
Chapter 1	Salvation Gift Package	19
Chapter 2	Salvation Tool Box	43
Chapter 3	The Blessing Thief	71
Chapter 4	Wolves in Sheep's Clothing	95
Chapter 5	Living as Heirs of the Most High	117
Chapter 6	Divine Partnership	143
Epilogue		*167*
	Children of The King	*167*
	Abundant Life	*187*

Foreword

In "Training to Reign with God, the Christian Guide to Spiritual Maturity" Dr. Marcia Vogl has condensed the knowledge she has gained through years of study, ministry and counseling experience, into an easy-to-read book. The book begins by establishing a clear picture of what a mature Christian disciple should look like and then provides a practical roadmap that, if followed, will prepare and equip you for a fulfilling and fruitful life. Using scripture, interesting stories that illustrate spiritual concepts, and her own experiences as a Christian counselor and Bible teacher, the lessons in this book are crafted to lead the reader at any level of maturity into a closer relationship with Christ.

"Training to Reign with God, the Christian Guide to Spiritual Maturity" is a book with sound and effective strategies that work. These same teachings have been employed by Marcia in seminars, classes and individual counseling sessions attended by members of our local church. I have personally witnessed individuals who were diligent to apply what they learned from Marcia become increasingly transformed into more mature disciples enjoying greater levels of freedom and fruitfulness.

Whether your need is personal or for a corporate study setting, *Training to Reign With God* is the discipleship resource you are looking for.

Pastor David Langeland
Safe Harbor Church

Introduction

At age 39, I lived what seemed to be an idyllic life, with three children, a loving husband, a beautiful home, with no financial worries. The last thing I expected was to quickly descend into depression. From being highly accomplished and energetic I sank into helplessness. For three weeks, the Lord had put me face to face with the people He wanted me to help while being one of them. I was not there as a psychiatrist, or a social worker, or nurse. While in this psychiatric unit, I met many hurting and desperate people I had only heard about but never met. The suicidal, addicted, demonically oppressed, and those saddled with infirmity all crossed my path.

During my two-year recovery period, I walked closely with the Lord relying on Him every moment of the day until walking with Him became the norm. Then I pursued studies in practical ministry partnering with others to pray, to deliver, and to strengthen the weak.

I began with individual personal ministry then discovered many more needed this kind of caring. This is was not Bible study but a more personal lifestyle fellowship. Individuals do not need to understand theological rhetoric to implement a Biblical lifestyle. My home church did not have the resources or manpower to offer this kind of small group ministry. I started developing workshops so more people could receive basic ministry offered on the personal prayer ministry platform. Material for these workshops became useful to many and in demand that I began writing books for more people to benefit.

Now, having more than 30 years of experience in pastoral counseling, teaching, and mentoring, I am focused on ministering to the-man-in-the pew, those searching for God in everyday life, and leaders who often have to stand alone. I guide and encourage developing leaders in the church and in the marketplace.

Great Bible stories tell how God directed the lives of saints and rogues. Modern Christian testimonials speak of how Jesus impacted their lives.

Mature Christians are like mature fruit trees that bear good fruit and seeds for future generations of trees. They plant seeds of wisdom, caution, advice, and even joy to other Christians discovering the Lord and the next generation. In my estimation, Chuck Pierce, Isaac Petrie, and Cindy Jacobs are mature Christians who pour out to others while maintaining their humanness. Other not-so-famous mature Christians to me are my accountant, book coaches, and gym trainers. This book is about becoming a mature Christian so you, too, can live a fruitful life and be a positive impact on future generations.

As a pastoral counselor for 30 years, I have heard the request for the "magical" life of peace where there are no conflicts. I cannot deliver that, but I can lead you into Christian maturity. My ministry includes personal prayer counseling to help you delve into traumas, wounds, and bondages of the past that hold you captive. I partner with the Holy Spirit to discover the source of your pain and how to untangle you from its web. The result is the freedom to walk in the prosperous and productive life that God had originally planned for you. This process may take many sessions but certainly not years. God does quick work when you seek His solutions. Things move even faster when you incorporate His principles into your life daily.

Francine's story is one of many I have had the privilege to unfold. It shows that God loves people, and He will go to great lengths to let them know he loves them and is available to them. He wants the best for them. And He wants the best for you.

Francine's story

Francine sat across me in hopelessness as she related her story. She was celebrating one year of sobriety. But was it really celebrating? Alcohol had wrecked her life since she was a teenager. She was married to an alcoholic. They fought, and he was verbally abusive and sometimes violent. With no money for an apartment, they lost custody of their two children, and all her dreams were shattered. She wanted to be a nurse. Loved being a mom. Loved her husband dearly, but they were stuck. They were now living at her parent's home in one room where their children were under the legal custody of her parents. She was a Christian but lost sight of the Christian life. Sobriety through Alcoholic Anonymous was her first step.

Francine wanted more than sobriety. She wanted life. She knew she made some stupid choices. I led her to first forgive herself for making bad choices. She forgave her husband for making bad choices too. Once the self-condemnation was removed, she had a glimmer of hope at the end of the tunnel. Her recovery was not instant, nor was it an easy road.

Francine fell in love with Jesus and started going to church again. She surprised her family and some friends thought she was a lost cause.

We had many prayer sessions where I encouraged her and we prayed for the guidance of the Holy Spirit. We also went through repentance and forgiveness through all the stages of her life. I walked her through deliverance from alcohol. Then she received inner healing for her soul. Each session made her stronger and more resolved to change. With determination, she completed nursing school for her LVN and RN certificates. While working in a rehab recovery clinic, she touched others with her recovery story. She prayed with them and taught them to repent and forgive. She now could earn a substantial income in her nursing profession.

Her husband had quit his desk job and wandered in and out of other jobs. Finally, he found a job in a botanical nursery. He became alive in the outdoors, and his creativity was awakened. He quit drinking.

With creative projects, he was excited to work again. He found favor with his bosses.

Both being sober and working together, they saved enough money to get their apartment and reclaim their children. They moved to a more rural area that suited their personalities and are loving parents to their children.

For Francine, salvation was indeed being saved from a trapped life. It was through Jesus that she was rescued and transformed.

God never changed his mind about us being above and not beneath, reigning over the earth. We are "to hold the dominion, sway, or influence of one resembling a monarch." You reign when you hold a high position as the recognized leader in your field, such as the "Reigning tennis champion, the reigning Miss America, or the reigning Olympic Gold Medalist." The Christian who reigns is the leader over his territory given by God. It could be a home, company, or personal accomplishment. You must prepare in skill and mentality to ascend to a position of leadership and accomplishment. All reigning sports figures train to get where they are as individuals or teams. They train, nonetheless.

In this book, I address maturity in your Christian faith so that you can reign over your life. Plain and simple terms without too much Bible-ese or theological jargon should make it easy to understand. Because the principles are based on Scripture, I have given you the Biblical references for you to look up for yourself. I use a combination of Biblical scenarios and imaginary stories to illustrate truths along with direct teachings and personal experiences. I assure you they are keys to your spiritual growth.

A blessed life is crafted with intentional life choices. It is not by accident or luck. In the following pages, I will share with you what intentional choices you will have to make to stay on the path with God. They are not rules and regulations but principles applied to your life. Biblical principles operate at all times for everyone.

Because I believe God has impacted my life to bear good fruit before delving into Biblical principles, the Prologue will give you samples of my experiences of God-impacting my life. God showed himself as my Protector, Provider, Rewarder, and Joy Giver.

Chapters 1 and 2 reveal the gift of Salvation and how you can benefit. When you have and stand for something of great worth, there will be opposition. Chapters 3 and 4 will spell out for you how the devil will try to steal your blessings. You will have opposition, but you will know how to stand. Chapters 5 and 6 lay out principles to live by with practical tips to apply. Again, these are not rules. They are the frameworks through which you can define your life choices. These will till the soil you are growing in to bring you to a mature fruit-bearing tree. You can expect God to respond, and he will work on your behalf. I hope that The Epilogue will encourage you as you read more stories of how the Lord continues to pour into me and those around me.

I suggest you read this book in order as each concept methodically builds your understanding of the Christian life with personal reflection guides, examples of effectual prayer, and practical steps for progress.

Finally, you, as a finite being, will not be able to comprehend an infinite God, yet you can relate to Him. You must learn to stretch your imagination to accept a God of eternity. Your life and mine are just slivers of time in eternity. Our slivers are very important to all who live in the presence of God. No one is expendable in God's eyes. We are all dearly loved and have a purpose designated by Him. My destiny connects to yours in a way I may not understand, but I know this because He loves us both and you are reading this book.

When you finish reading this book:
- You will have practical spiritual tools to live out your Salvation.
- You will be wise to perceive the opposition you will face.
- You will have a framework for making good life choices with Jesus Christ as your partner.

- You will bear good fruit in your garden of life, enjoying the beauty and sharing your fruit with others.
- You will be trained to reign over your life and your assigned territory.

Prologue

Remembering is the ability to re-member or put things back together again. The members come into unity to make a whole. There is such power in remembering the goodness of God and how he so lovingly and sneakily works in our lives when we permit Him. You might ask Him to work in your life, but if you don't permit Him to do it His way, you might be disappointed.

Foresight with God is obedience, believing He is a good God and will not steer you into failure. Your obedience will unlock whatever provision is necessary, whether natural or supernatural. Hindsight is praise and thanksgiving. Each experience increased my faith that God is there working behind the scenes for my good and will be in the next situation.

These are short stories of some experiences when God showed up in wonderful ways in my life. I can't say I worked for them or earned them. I believe they resulted from living with Him, trusting Him, and nurturing the desire to let Him be God.

Graduate School

So Abraham called that place
The Lord Will Provide. And to this day it is said,
"On the mountain of the Lord it will be provided."

(Genesis 22:14)

I opened the letter with great anticipation. "You are admitted to the Masters of Science program in the graduate school at the University of Illinois." Wow! I was the first in my family to go to graduate school, much less in another state.

This was 1967, before email, the internet, and cheap phone calls. I had poured over brochures to choose a graduate school for my Master's degree. I had sent my application by mail without guarantee that it would get there on time. After all, I was across the Pacific Ocean in Hawaii and the university was in the midwest of the USA. A campus visit was out of the question. As far as I was concerned, it was another country. I had completed my Bachelor of Education in Music, but I had not left the state of Hawaii throughout my 23 years of growing up. This was going to be an adventure. The University of Illinois was well known for its music education faculty who were the authors of the books used in the public schools. I was looking forward to studying under these noted instructors.

The practical part of attending graduate school so far away from home included living in a dorm, flying more than 6,000 miles, making new friends, and learning to live on my own. The University of Hawaii was conveniently within walking distance of my parents' home. I worked two part-time jobs to help pay for the college tuition and books, while I lived at home.

My parents were very supportive but could not finance graduate school. They were willing to take out a student loan to cover the out-of-state fee, tuition, room and board, and air travel, not to mention basic living expenses. This was my first trip to the mainland.

Teamed up with another music student going to the U of I as an undergraduate, I started on the adventure. Fortunately, the "coconut wireless," or the Hawaii college student network, went into action. A law school student from Hawaii agreed to pick us up at the airport and deliver us to our respective dorms.

As travel neophytes, Patty and I took the one-hour LAX layover to be "Hawaiian time,"—we wait for you. She and I went to breakfast at the airport restaurant and returned to the gate in one hour, only to watch our plane going down the runway. The gate personnel was gracious in assuring us we could get on the next flight to Chicago and make our connection to Midway airport. Patty worried that her violin would be stolen as she had it as carry-on luggage.

As promised, we caught the next flight, and all our belongings were waiting for us at the gate except for our flower leis. The violin was safe and sound. When we arrived at midway Airport, Wesley was waiting for us and drove us to our dorms. Tired from the trip, I didn't settle in but just crashed. The next day, Tina, another music graduate student from the University of Hawaii, contacted me.

"Go apply for the Resident Assistant job!" she urged.

"What is that?" I asked.

"You live in an undergrad dorm as a floor counselor. The dean is looking for one Resident Assistant from each state in the union. There is no Hawaii RA yet. She'll like you and give you the position. I have one, but I'm from Vietnam," she said excitedly.

At the Housing Office, I was ushered into the Dean's office. After she asked me about my life in Hawaii, she presented the job requirements. It seemed being accepted as a graduate student was good enough credentials.

She proceeded to describe the job. "The position open is in Allen Hall on the Rehab floor. These women are physically disabled but capable of attending college. Each one has an AB (Able-Bodied) roommate.

Your job would be to be the floor counselor as the "go-to person" should there be any difficulty. Do you think you can do that?"

"Doesn't sound too difficult. I'm up for it."

"We can take a tour before you decide. One woman is a polio victim and sleeps in an iron lung, another has cerebral palsy and types with a pencil in her teeth. Ten wheelchairs are whizzing around. Does that make you uncomfortable?"

"No, I'm not afraid of wheelchairs."

"If you take this position, you will have a private room on the first floor that is wheelchair accessible. We will waive the out-of-state fee, the tuition and cover your room and board. You will have a pass to eat in any dining room on campus and receive a stipend of $85 a month for incidentals."

I could barely take this all in. The loan my parents took would not be needed. I'll have a private room for just being around.

After touring the dorm, I didn't see anything that would stop me from doing this. The women were mostly freshmen, nice as ever. The iron-lung gal only slept in it and had a caregiver roommate. The others were whizzing around freely in their wheelchairs. I was shown my room which had a private bath with a bathtub. All the mirrors, counters, and bed were low, set for wheelchairs. Perfect for shorty me. The Dean said she was hoping she would have a wheelchair counselor, but none applied. School was starting in 2 days, and she needed to fill the position. Here I was!

Wesley helped me move in, and I was set up for school with new friends. The RA staff was a diverse group of women with many majors. Most were in psychology to be counselors, one artist, and one a scientist. I was the only musician. One was from Egypt, an African American from Chicago, and variations of Caucasian. I was the only Chinese. I was welcomed warmly at the first evening meeting. We all had assigned evening office duty in the counseling office. The main duty was to "be present and lock the doors at night." Most students who sought us out were freshmen who just wanted to talk about adjusting to college life and maybe their boyfriends. Nothing life-threatening.

Remember, this was before email or cheap phone calls. I sent my parents a "telegram," which was a message in twenty-five words or less. That was the cheapest, fast communication. "Got job as RA (stop). Do not need money for tuition (stop). Everything is fine. (stop) Will write. (stop)." Then I wrote them a long letter hoping it would get there within the week.

The young women on my floor welcomed me with open arms and hearts. They introduced me to the world of Gizz Kids. Gizz Kids are those who depend on gizmos such as waste bags, artificial legs or arms, wheelchairs of all kinds, and other aids for the disabled. They introduced me to wheelchair basketball. I rode the handicap bus with them and went to their outings. This was a world I had no idea about. They were just real people who had physical handicaps and persevered to overcome them. Some took more than an hour just to get ready for class. A few even invited me to their homes for the holidays.

God not only relieved me of the college financial burden, but He enriched my life beyond my wildest imagination and at no cost. I was paid to work on my "free" Master's Degree.

He enriched my life beyond my wildest imagination.

Vanagon Rescue

For he will command his angels concerning you to guard you in all your ways. (Psalm 91:11)

We were on a family trip driving north on Highway #99 to Fresno, California, with our three children in our 1990 Volkswagen Vanagon. The children were in the back seat, with one in the far back cargo area. This was before the days of mandatory seat belts. Suddenly, from the cargo area, we heard:

"There's black smoke coming out the back of the car!"

A quick look confirmed the alarm. We pulled off the highway in what seemed like the middle of nowhere. We hustled the kids out of the car and stood afar off on the side of the road, hoping the car would not burst into flames.

Almost immediately, a AAA (Automobile Club of CA) patrol car pulled up behind us. An agent got out of his car.

"Look like you got some trouble. I was following you and saw the smoke."

I have never seen this kind of AAA patrol car before. He radioed for a tow truck. (This was before the days of cell phones.) We were 5 miles from the town of Wasco, which is midway between Interstate 5 and Highway #99. We nervously waited for the tow truck to arrive.

The tow truck was the old pull-you-along kind, not the new flatbed models. It was driven by a chatty old man who hooked up our van. We wondered whether we would be left on the side of the road since there were 5 of us.

"No worries. We'll all fit in the front seat," said the driver confidently. We piled onto the seat with the children on our laps for the 5-mile ride to Wasco. There was only one gas station in town where the car could be towed with only one mechanic on duty. This was a late Saturday morning, so needless to say, the shop was busy. With a disabled car, we had no choice but to wait.

The kids and I went across the street to the Kentucky Fried Chicken for some lunch while my husband waited to get the verdict on the car. While at lunch, we prayed, "Lord, please fix our car. Keep us safe. We want to finish our trip." That was the eloquence of three young children.

After almost an hour, we learned that the part needed was not available at the only auto parts store in town—after all, this was VW Vanagon. The young man, who looked about 17 years old, said he would do his best to get us to at least Fresno, where the Volkswagen dealer might have the part. It had something to do with the water-cooling system, which needed a special gasket. He advised us not to let the car overheat and to carry water to keep this water-box engine cool.

After another hour, we were off, keeping our fingers crossed and carrying a jug of water. We stopped at every rest stop on the way to cool the car off and check the water. At the rest stop before Fresno, we all got out to stretch and check the car. All of us were looking under the car for any leaks. While doing so, a retired-age couple in a large Cadillac drove up next to us and asked if we needed help.

"We're looking for leaks, so our car does not burn up. We just need a temporary fix till we get to the dealer in Fresno," my husband explained.

"We're going right past there. This is a big car. We can fit you all in and drop you off there."

"No, we can't leave the car here. We'll just mosey along carefully."

"Well, we will be happy to follow you until you get to Fresno. That way, if it does break down, we will be there to rescue you."

"That will be great. Thank you."

We made it to the Fresno exit. As we were turning off the freeway, my husband asked me to get the car license plates so he could write the people a thank you letter. As the car drove past us, the people waved. It was a new car with no plates or markings.

By the time we got into Fresno, the Volkswagen dealer was already closed, and we would have to wait until Tuesday as Monday was a holiday, which is why we were on this trip in the first place. We proceeded with our plans for the weekend, driving the car carefully, going only short distances so as not to overheat it. We had a good time checking out museums and visiting with relatives.

Work and school resumed on Tuesday, so we had to get home by Monday night. We decided to take the chance driving 350 miles home, risking a possible breakdown again. We drove carefully, stopping at all rest stops to let the car cool off. We made it home without an incident.

On Tuesday, I took the car to the local dealer to be fixed.

The service department manager advised, "The part needed is an unusual part that we do not keep in stock. It has to be ordered and will take a week to arrive. Meanwhile, it looks like the fix that was made is good enough to last the week if you drive it carefully. Make an appointment to bring the car back next week."

As I reflected on that weekend's adventure, these questions popped up in my mind.

Where did the AAA rescue car come from?

How did the tow truck driver get there so fast?

How did that young mechanic know how to fix a car he had never worked on before?

Who were those people who followed us to Fresno, giving us cover?

How did we get home without another breakdown?

How can this last another week?

He is a good God! He commanded His angels to guard us.

Angels come in all shapes and sizes and are disguised as helpers.

Time For Others

Serve wholeheartedly, as if you were serving the Lord, not people, because you know that the Lord will reward each one for whatever good they do. (Ephesians 6:7-8)

The elderly woman was sitting outside the grocery store, fretting, nearly in tears.

"Can I help you?" I asked.

"No," sob, sob.

"What is the matter?"

"I called for a taxi to take me home, but I have been waiting for half an hour, and my ice cream is melting. I only live across the street, but I can't cross the street."

This store was fronted by a very busy street.

"May I help take you across?"

"I can't carry my groceries!"

"I can drive you there if you tell me where you live."

"You can't lift the groceries!"

"Let me try. My car is just a few steps away."

I picked up her two small bags of groceries, and after putting them in the trunk, I helped her into the car. She lived in the apartment complex across the street. I parked the car outside her unit and then proceeded to retrieve the groceries from the trunk as she led the way to the door. When I put the groceries on the counter inside the door, she said, "Wait," and handed me some money.

"That is not necessary. It was my pleasure to help. Save it for your next cab ride."

I was on my lunch hour when all this happened. This was the day before Thanksgiving, and I planned to quickly stop at the grocery store for a few last-minute things. Silly me! I returned to the grocery store to gather my items even though now my lunch hour was running out and the check-out lines were very long.

I looked at my watch and the three people ahead with full carts. I turned suddenly as I felt a tap on my shoulder. A grocery clerk ushered me to another register. I quickly moved as she opened up. As soon as I laid my purchases on the conveyer belt, she put up her "lane closed sign." I was out in a flash and was headed back to the office on time.

Rewards come in many forms. For me, this was a reward of time. I could have easily ignored the woman sitting outside. Many others did. Usually, an hour at lunch would not be time enough to do what I intended. Special treatment in the grocery store put me at the head of the line. I was rewarded for reaching out to help.

A Grandma's Joy

*He settles the childless woman in her home as
a happy mother of children.* (Psalm 113:9)

Things did not work out the way I envisioned them, but God knew our heart's desire and made a way through the impossible.

It is Thanksgiving time 2009. I am sitting in church holding my first grandson, Aidan, on my lap, with tears streaming down my face as we are singing, "How great is our God." I am reminded of how God is a faithful generational God.

When I was 29 years old, I had a face-off with cancer. Because I am now telling you this story, you know who won. That battle, however, left me unable to bear more children. Although we already had a son, we wanted to adopt more children to complete a family of three children. We told our friends we were looking to adopt a child. We were a mixed marriage between Chinese and Austrian. When the Vietnam War ended, and many refugees came to the USA, a person involved in placing Vietnamese children knew a couple who preferred to have their child adopted into an Asian family. We were the only Asian family he knew. Would we take this child? Of course, we would. At two days old, James became ours in September 1975.

A few years later, we searched for a daughter. The Asian countries stopped allowing their children to be adopted away from their native land. To find another Asian child would be difficult and would take perhaps five years. After submitting our application, we settled in for the wait. Within 30 days, we got a call to adopt a Korean girl age 2 ½. She was brought to the USA before Korea closed its doors to foreign adoptions. The adopting mother had fallen very ill and could not care for her, so she was to be placed again. The former family had two young boys the same ages as ours, so the agency thought this would be the perfect transition. Within a week, we had a new daughter. This young girl grew up, married, and now is the mother of Aidan, the grandson sitting on my lap.

When I was 29, the joy of being a grandmother was in the distance, but I knew it could happen. The Enemy tried to steal that "grandmother's joy" from me, *but God* had it in store for me.

(*reprint permission by christiandevotions.us*)

CHAPTER 1

Salvation Gift Package

Salvation is God's escorted plan for you to live out your purpose under Jesus Christ. Salvation is not a "one-way ticket" to heaven after death, as has been purported. That would be trying to take earth to heaven. That would not make heaven better. Through Jesus Christ, we join Christians to bring the Kingdom of Heaven to earth to make earth better. Salvation is a gift package from God for everyone of any age who focuses on fulfilling his destiny regardless of opposition in the world. This Salvation is not a one-time event but an ongoing process of being saved from the world's torrential flood. Success is yours when you accept the gift package of healing, restoration, and prosperity, all included.

Restoration is More than 911

"But I will restore you to health and heal your wounds," declares the Lord, "because you are called an outcast, Zion for whom no one cares." (Jeremiah 30:17)

"Charlie, better come quickly. We got a mean one here by the back fence." Charlie was the animal control officer hailed by the school janitor. When Charlie arrived, he found a mixed breed pit bull pacing against the school fence. It snarled at him looking to escape or attack. Charlie has handled tough ones before, so he skillfully calmed the dog and quickly looped him with his leash. Even though the dog writhed and yelped, Charlie carefully put him in the truck for a trip to the local shelter. Meanwhile, in another cage in the truck was a schnauzer cowering and shaking in the corner.

At the shelter, Charlie carefully put each dog in a separate cage to be later examined by the vet and cared for by the staff.

Joey was assigned to the pit bull. He spent the next few days winning the friendship of this mean and scared dog he named Butch. Butch was fed and eventually bathed and groomed. Joey slowly made friends with Butch until he was allowed to touch him without danger. Over the following days, Butch learned to trust Joey and the other trainers. When his fears were calmed, he could take instruction on a leash. He could play and meet strangers without snarling. It became a frolicking fun event when visitors came looking to rescue a dog. Dogs were adoptable only after being able to trust new owners.

Meanwhile, the schnauzer was curled up in the corner whining. She had been underfed and had sores on her skin. She was suffering from neglect. Veronica, her vet staff assignee, named her Sweetpea and carefully tended to her sores, fed her nutritious meals, and played with her, bringing her out of her fearful shell. In time, her sores healed, she gained weight, and she was willing to play and be handled on a leash. She then became as playful as a puppy.

Both dogs were later adopted. Butch, the pit bull, became a search and rescue partner to a fireman handler. They built up a strong bond of obedience and love. The little schnauzer, Sweetpea, became the joy of a little girl's heart. They too had a relationship of obedience, love, and fun.

These were "rescue dogs" prepared for good homes. These dogs learned to eventually trust their new masters, bringing joy to many others.

Similarly, people can be mean and ugly due to past experiences or meek and cowering if neglected. They need a rescuer or a Savior. If you have experienced abuse, pain, and sorrow making you mean and angry, you need a rescuer. If you have been neglected, you also need a rescuer. All Mankind, lost in the world's clutches, need a rescuer or a Savior to feed, heal, and love us.

The rescuer of Mankind is Jesus Christ.

Eternity is God's Clock

*Do not fear, for I have redeemed you;
I have summoned you by name; you are mine.*

(Isaiah 43:1)

God sees time through eternity. Our time clock is in hours, days, and years. The Father, Son, and Holy Spirit were in existence before the beginning of time in the world.

God, the Creator, made a human out of the dust of the earth and breathed His own life into Man, making him a companion. In Genesis 2, we learn that God gave Mankind (Adam) dominion over the whole earth. Adam named all the creatures. He had dominion over the fish of the sea. He could eat anything in the garden. All was beautiful and luscious. The only restricted item was fruit from the Tree of the Knowledge of Good and Evil. This restriction was the test of obedience. This was not poisoned fruit that would kill their bodies. Would Adam and Eve put aside their personal reasoning to obey God? The fruit was beautiful, luscious to the sight, and would taste good, but so were the other fruits in the garden. Why was this one on the restricted tree so attractive?

Satan lured Eve and Adam into disobeying God by focusing on what was forbidden and not what was graciously given. As with Adam and Eve, Satan constantly attempts to turn Mankind's thoughts away from God's blessings. Why do we always want the things we are not supposed to have? If hiking alone is dangerous for you, why do you want to go alone? If overeating is bad for you, why do you want to overeat? Satan knows how to lure you into bad choices.

To God's sorrow, Adam and Eve chose to listen to the voice of Satan, who led them into disobedience. Knowing Mankind would have a hard time resisting Satan's lures and lies, God had a rescue plan. God had to rescue Mankind because Mankind could not redeem itself. The redemption price must be a perfect Man of human flesh who must someday redeem all humanity for all time.

"To redeem" means to recover something or regain possession by paying the full price, thus erasing all debt. A redeemed mortgage is one paid in full. My children took aluminum cola cans to the redemption center, where cans destined for the trash dump were redeemed or taken back and given value. People caught in the traps of sin are headed for the trash heap. The cross of Jesus Christ is the redemption center. He pays the redemption price to recover you and restore your value.

For years, men sacrificed birds, bulls, and goats as redemption for sin, but those could not redeem a person. Mankind can only be redeemed by the shedding of pure blood of humanity that Adam had at creation. God had to produce a human of the same flesh as Adam with original purity.

The Bible reveals that God's plan for redemption would take place over thousands of years. This may seem like a long time, but to the God of eternity, it was relatively quick.

God is a Planner

"For I know the plans I have for you," declares the Lord, "plans to prosper you and not to harm you, plans to give you hope and a future." (Jeremiah 29:11)

God is faithful to carry out His plan to bring Salvation to Mankind. The prophets foretold it. Those willing to wait and listen saw his hand.

God prepared for the Messiah's appearance on earth for centuries. The Jews were waiting for a promised Messiah for more than 400 years. The hope was passed down through the generations that God would send a Savior to rescue them from the oppression of the various dynasties that swept over their country. The descendants of Abraham carried in their hearts the promise God made to Abraham centuries earlier that He would build a great nation based on Abraham's obedience and faithfulness to God. They would worship and obey God, the Creator. They would be called Hebrews and would be the lineage of generations to produce the Messiah.

Zechariah was the high priest about a year before Jesus was born. He and his wife Elizabeth were righteous in the sight of God, but childless. They probably had given up hope, as their bodies were beyond the age of procreation. But God answered their prayer by making it possible for them to bear a child in their old age. Their son, John the Baptist, would be the forerunner of the Messiah.

Mary, a young girl, was prepared by God to conceive His only Begotten Son. This son was made flesh through the womb of Mary by the power of the Holy Spirit. Jesus would have the same human flesh as Adam and the same God-spirit as Adam. The process was different, but the result was the same for a perfect exchange. God re-created a man like Adam through the womb of a woman.

As the story unfolds, Emperor Caesar Augustus demanded a census that required all families to travel to their historic town of lineage. There was no online census or census by mail at that time. People had to physically travel to the town of their ancestors. Mary and Joseph traveled to Bethlehem because they were descendants of King David. Mary birthed Jesus while they were in Bethlehem.

The birth of Jesus, the Messiah, would be good news for the whole world. However, God did not declare this through the mouths of men in the palaces, streets, and marketplaces. He sent angels to herald the good news to shepherds. Angelic appearance signaled this birth was something of God and not men's imagination. This awesome experience with the Messiah was mind-boggling. This was not a "conspiracy theory."

When Jesus was eight days old, his parents took him to the temple to be dedicated according to custom (Luke 2:25). God had promised elderly Simeon, a very devout and righteous man, that he would live long enough to see the Messiah with his own eyes, not just hope for him. Simeon entered the temple just as Mary and Joseph were bringing Jesus to be dedicated. He took the baby in his arms, proclaiming God's promise to him was fulfilled to see the promised Hope of Mankind.

The 84-year-old widow Anna, a prophetess, also waited faithfully in the temple to see the Messiah (Luke 2:36). How many thousands of babies had she seen in her 60 years in the temple? When she saw Jesus, even as an infant, she knew who he was and discreetly spread the news of hope to others.

Magi also followed a strange new star from as far as Persia. They surmised it signaled a King of great importance. These kings were seeking someone greater than themselves. We understand from the Bible that this journey took about two years, so Jesus was a toddler when they arrived. (This timing is not the compressed version found in the typical church Christmas play where the Magi kneel at the cradle of the newborn king.) The quest of the well-meaning and naïve Magi tipped off Herod that there was a child who would be a great King. Jealousy and fear put Herod on a murderous rampage to kill all male babies under two years old. Through a warning dream, God sent the baby and family fleeing to Egypt, where they stayed until Herod's death. The family returned to Israel to live as promised in the scriptures.

The boy Jesus probably celebrated Shabbat, the Sabbath, and the annual Hebrew festivals with his family. He was schooled in the scriptures and the Torah. Through historical accounts, we know he had a typical childhood with siblings carrying out the customs of the Hebrew people. As a young boy of Bar Mitzvah age, 13 years old, he lingered in the temple during the Passover celebration to discuss scripture with the elders (Luke 2:41-50). The hand of God was moving on this young boy, who could converse with the elders and the rabbis.

The adult Jesus followed his father Joseph's trade as a carpenter, so we know he worked with his hands. He interacted with the common folk.

At age 30, Jesus had his "coming out" party. He was set apart through the baptism of John the Baptist and the 40-day temptations in the wilderness. He was an approved Rabbi as he was given the Torah to read in the synagogue public worship. Jesus' voice had authority never before heard. From that time, He began to preach the Kingdom of God or the "Reign of God" that was coming. The current reign was the "Reign of Sin and Death." For three years, he taught and trained disciples to carry out the news of Salvation throughout the world. This was no small local movement. It started in a small region but was meant to cover the earth.

The culmination of the Salvation epic took place on Calvary when Jesus, age 33, was crucified in the cruelest, most despicable death known in the Roman Empire. The religious powers accused him of blasphemy because he claimed to be the Son of God. Such an outrageous claim deserved the death sentence. The synagogue leaders managed to convince the Roman government to convict Jesus of sedition by twisting His words against Him. He had obeyed God the Father explicitly in all things throughout his life. Perfect obedience made Him worthy to pay the price for the redemption of Mankind. His death seemed to be a tragic ending but was the greatest joy in all the world. After three days in a tomb, Jesus rose from the grave, overcoming death. He would never die again, but instead, he would return to the Father and the Holy Spirit to live for all Mankind for all time.

Adam's disobedience brought death to all Mankind. Jesus conquered death and restored life to Mankind. Each person can now choose to accept Jesus as Savior and live in the kingdom where God reigns. As He proclaimed, "The Kingdom of God is at hand!" No one is forced to accept this kingdom, but those who choose not to, miss out on a relationship with the Creator of the universe and eternal life.

Just as God orchestrated the appearance of Jesus, and He orchestrates events in your life today.

> **Miracles are being prepared and happening all the time.**

Some are hidden in plain sight. Your ability to perceive miracles is part of the "Salvation package." When you perceive miracles, you will live in them. He prepares the hearts and minds of people to be blessed. I believe that whenever you see the hand of God moving, a miracle is in the making.

Passover Fulfilled

"I have eagerly desired to eat this Passover with you before I suffer. For I tell you, I will not eat it again until it finds fulfillment in the kingdom of God." (Luke 22:15)

The Israelites had been in bondage in Egypt for 400 years. Knowing their plight under Pharaoh, God sent Moses to deliver them from Egypt into Canaan as promised to Abraham. As much as Moses implored Pharaoh to let the people leave Egypt to worship God, Pharaoh remained stubborn. This was a spiritual war. God the "I AM" opposed the gods of Egypt through ten plagues as opportunities for him to "let the people go!" But Pharaoh would not. Finally, the last plague was the death of the firstborn of men and animals.

After Moses decreed the death of the firstborn, God instituted Passover as protection of his people through the Passover Lamb. The Israelites were instructed to slay a yearling lamb, put the blood on the doorposts, eat the roasted lamb with the family, stay indoors, and get ready to leave Egypt immediately afterward because Pharaoh would finally permit them to leave. The death angel would "Passover" those homes with the blood on the doorposts, which signified that the inhabitants were God's people. This was the first Passover celebration. This feast was ordained to be celebrated throughout history as a remembrance of God's deliverance.

Historically, whenever the Israelites strayed from God by moving into idolatry or were exiled to a foreign land, the Lord would call them back by reminding them to celebrate Passover. Passover is God's promise of deliverance from their enemies and the return under God's reign.

Up to the last Passover celebrated by Jesus before his death, Passover was a *promise* for God's deliverance from their enemies. Few realized the real enemy was sin and death. Most thought the Roman Empire was their enemy, as was Pharaoh in Egypt.

All previous Passover Feasts were prophecies of what God was *going to do*. This last one at the end of Jesus' life with His disciples was "the real thing." At the first Passover in Egypt, the blood of the lamb was smeared on the doorposts, so the death angel would "pass over" that house. When Jesus said, "**This** is my body," He was ***the Passover Lamb*** speaking. The cup that Jesus offered was His blood poured out to remove the penalty of sin. Death will "pass over." What the modern church celebrates as ***The Last Supper*** is the fulfilled Passover.

Jesus rose from the dead because death had no power to hold Him. He rose with a resurrected body that could go through walls, appear and disappear anytime, yet He could eat and drink. When He first appeared to the apostles, he asked for something to eat, proving he was not a ghost but real flesh and blood. He invited Thomas to touch the wounds in his hands and side to prove He was real. Four days later, He walked on the road to Emmaus with two disciples. He broke the bread and drank wine with them, signifying that the Kingdom of God was fulfilled. It was through Passover that the disciples recognized him (Luke 24:30).

The Kingdom of God is fulfilled in you because Jesus' body was broken and His blood was shed to be ***the Passover Lamb*** sacrifice that delivers you from sin and death. His resurrection proves He lives even after the death of the flesh. He gives you life.

Today we celebrate The Communion or the Last Supper because it is the completed Passover sacrifice. Jesus is the "real Passover Lamb." The Israelites did not stay in Egypt after the death angel passed over. They started the journey to the Promised Land. Every time we celebrate the "Passover" or Communion, the next step is to "pass over" into our future. Do not stay in the land of slavery.

Debt Paid in Full

... and (they) must confess the sin they have committed. They must make full restitution for the wrong they have done, add a fifth of the value to it and give it all to the person they have wronged. (Numbers 5:7)

The law of restitution is in operation over all the earth, whether you believe in it or not. In the scripture above, the law of restitution is spelled out in application to theft, injury, and property damage. Restitution requires the offender to replace or restore what has been damaged or injured to the original condition before it was damaged, with a penalty of 20% value. This law ensures that balance is restored and no debt is left unpaid.

At a lovely banquet, I left my evening bag on the seat while I went to the buffet. When I returned, to my surprise, I found the waiter wiping up my seat, table place, and my purse. The guest sitting next to me had accidentally knocked over her drink, drenching my place, seat, and evening bag. She was very apologetic and offered to replace it. A few days later, I received a note of apology, and a check for what she guessed was the cost of replacing my evening bag. The money was more than sufficient. This was a case of total restitution paid.

My husband got into an auto accident in his less-than-one-year-old sedan. The broadside impact released the safety airbags. The car was "totaled" because the cost of repairing the body damage and resetting the airbags was greater than the fair value of the car. Consequently, he was authorized to purchase a new car that was better than the one that was lost. Restitution satisfied the debt.

When you forgive the offending party, you open the way for the Lord to provide restitution. As long as we are dealing with things that can be replaced, restitution is possible. However, had my husband's accident caused bodily injury, the one who caused the accident (or his insurance company) would be required to pay the total medical costs involved and perhaps damages for suffering. If there was irreparable damage, such as a crippled arm, or blindness, no amount of money could repair or replace the arm or eye. While an injured party has a right to restitution from the offending party, what happens when restitution from the offender is impossible because no amount of money can replace what was lost? How does the law of restitution operate in these cases?

When you forgive, the restitution is covered by Jesus through the riches of His grace. For example, the following prayer could be said:

**"Lord, I forgive Andrew for causing the accident that blinded my left eye. He does not have to make it up to me. He owes me no restitution, no apology, no reasons, no explanations, and no excuses.
I choose to release him 100%.
I look to you to be my restitution."**

At a luncheon, a plate slipped from the waiter's hand and gravy splashed on my silk blouse. As much as he apologized, my silk blouse was ruined. He did not offer to pay, nor did I want to complain to the management. I forgave him and did not mourn over the loss of my silk blouse. Weeks later, a woman I did not know gave me a silk blouse, nicer than the one that was ruined. She said, "I bought this on clearance for myself, but after I brought it home, I realized it's too small for me. I believe it's your size. Would you like it? You may have it." I believe it was through the work of the Holy Spirit that I received restitution for my ruined blouse.

Jesus takes away the sting of the offense, and the way is opened for God to intervene and provide restitution in ways you could not imagine.

A job you never considered opens up, you meet the love of your life, you build lasting friendships with other disabled people, and, as a consequence, you discover beautiful things about yourself.

Do not look to the source of your hurt to be your source of restitution.

Jesus provides your restitution. This too, is part of your Salvation gift package.

Be Reconciled

"But I want you to know that the Son of Man has authority on earth to forgive sins." (Luke 5:24)

Unforgiveness is probably the most insidious spiritual hook on people. Years have been wasted when children don't forgive their parents for mistakes or fail in their expectations. The young boy whose dad could not play baseball with him will forever blame his dad for the failure to be a baseball star. The young girl who wanted to be a ballerina blames her mother for not giving her ballet lessons. Regardless of the circumstances, the youngsters cannot see past their expectations. They hold unforgiveness in their hearts.

Sisters who have had a spat over boyfriends, money, or "who was dad's favorite" will have unforgiveness as a wedge between them for years. The blame game can last a lifetime if you refuse to forgive. Forgiving can be tricky and elusive. You can think or believe you have forgiven but, in reality, you have not. Without total forgiveness, the link of sin between you and the other party will linger on.

The first step to forgiving is to admit you have been hurt. Refusing to accept you have been hurt is denial. Such statements as "It's ok," "I can take it," or "He didn't mean it" do not address the fact that you were hurt. Because your mind works so quickly, you can short circuit your emotions concerning the hurt or offense. If you collect all the remarks, deeds, and actions that offended you, you will become a time bomb. Each offense shortens the fuse. Forgiving is the way to diffuse the time bomb and get rid of it entirely.

It is more difficult to forgive an "invisible" offense than a blatant one because the evidence is elusive. Gossip, inferences, and allusions are invisible. "She said that…, they thought that…" statements are loaded with explosives. "You think that you're always right" is an explosive inference. Any kind of accusation, founded or unfounded, adds to your unforgiveness arsenal.

Someone arriving late, a glib remark, a crude joke, or a sarcastic remark sits like trash on your pathway. Quickly forgive someone for being offensive. This does not mean you have to condone their behavior or continue to accept their "trash," but you give yourself the freedom not to store their trash.

Five tentacles need to be cut in the process of forgiving.

1. **Expecting restitution.** The offender should provide some sort of compensation. You long for compensation for the hurt of a broken toe. Money and paid medical bills can try to compensate, but they don't. Even if that is provided, you are left dealing with your pain which can morph into resentment or anger. Any discomfort or disability, as a result, will get larger each day.

2. If restitution is not forthcoming, you look for a verbal statement of **apology** to soothe your hurt. "I'm sorry I ran over your toe," or "I'm sorry I injured you." An apology is great, but it does not heal the broken toe, nor does it make up for the inconveniences and pain you suffer.

3. If an apology is not forthcoming, which frequently happens when the offender does not know there was an offense, you want a **reason why** they hurt you. Whatever the reason, it really won't heal your hurt. "I wasn't paying attention," or "I lost control of the bike," will not heal your broken toe.

4. When a reason is not provided, you look for an **explanation** of facts and figures. "The bike was traveling at 20 miles an hour, and you were standing by the post. The force of the bike on your toe broke it." Explanations will not heal your broken toe.

5. When no explanation is forthcoming, you wait for an **excuse**. "I was rushing because my alarm clock did not ring." Now it's

the alarm clock's fault. Your broken toe is still not healed and your anger is rising. As a last resort, you make an excuse *for* the offending party with "He's having a bad day," as you limp away, muttering expletives under your breath.

To completely and truly forgive, you need to let go of all the links of offense and be set free from the five tentacles. (**R.A.R.E.Ex**) This is the prayer:

> **"Lord, I forgive Tim for riding his bike over my foot, breaking my toe. He does not owe me anything (restitution). He does not have to make it up to me. He does not have to apologize, give me a reason, give me an explanation, nor make any excuses. I forgive him 100% and release him from the sin-link with me. Amen."**

When you have been offended by something blatant, be specific in how you felt and perceived the situation, no matter how silly it sounds. Here are some common ones.

- I forgive the doctor for being too busy to take my calls.
- I forgive my father for not coming to my baseball games.
- I forgive my boss for not recognizing my extra efforts.
- I forgive my daughter for not calling on my birthday.

Forgiving is a choice. Forgiving any offense will free YOU from grudges, resentment, judgment, bitterness, envy, or malice.

Forgiving is the best medicine for a grumpy attitude, hurt feelings, and old resentments. As a little girl, my mother brewed Chinese herbal tea to cure a nagging cough. All I needed was a few gulps. It was bitter and nasty tasting. She tried to make it better with honey, raisins, and even sugar, but it was still nasty tasting. As much as I protested, she insisted I drink it. After much protestation, I would eventually get down the small gulps. As if by magic, the next morning, I would be well without the cough or cold. Had I moved my *will* and *chosen* to drink this bitter tea, I could have saved myself a lot of grief! Sometimes forgiving is like bitter tea that will be the cure for your angst. You don't want to do it, but it is the cure!

Forgiving and being forgiven are part of your Salvation life gift. God commands, not suggests, you forgive. Forgiving is by obedient **choice,** not feeling. You will not know real freedom until you forgive. All your rationalizing and emotional moaning and groaning are for naught.

Remember R.A.R.E.Ex (Restitution, Apology, Reasons, Explanations, Excuses) are the keys to total forgiveness and freedom.

Forgive without delay to be free from toxic relationships. Forgiving will remove the cloud of old incidents that haunt you. Who or what do you need to forgive? Be specific. Do it now without delay.

Realignment with God

"Repent, for the Kingdom of God is at hand."

(Matthew 4:17)

After being tempted by the devil in the wilderness, Jesus proclaimed the admonition to repent. This is a command, not a suggestion. The Kingdom of God is the realm where God's will and glory are normal for life. Repentance is a key to this Kingdom.

Repentance will remove the weight of guilt and shame. Repenting is not feeling sorry. Repenting is not feeling bad. Repenting is not "wishing it weren't that way." Repenting *is* admitting before God anything that does not align with Him and his Word so that the way will be open for behavioral change.

Here are five common ways to be out of alignment with God.

1. *The sins of Commission* are acts carried out not according to God's character or laws, such as theft, lying, murder, and fornication. Your behavior reflects whether your mind and heart are in sync with God. If you found a wallet on the floor of a grocery store, what would you do? Would you give it to the management "as is," or would you first keep all the cash?

2. *The sins of Omission* are those failures to do what should have been done. Failing to pay bills on time, not meeting deadlines, or failing to show up for a meeting can bring harm to yourself and others. Failing to honor an institution, person or event promotes an atmosphere of discord. The courts of law require honor from the litigants and lawyers. There is a proper way to address the judge and a proper demeanor that shows respect for the rule of law. Those who do not comply trespass with the sin of omission.

3. *The sins of the Mind* include thoughts and attitudes contrary to God's will, such as planning criminal activity, lying to deceive, or providing false evidence. A chain of lies and deception can go on endlessly. A man who cheats on his wife lies about his "business meetings." Then he has to lie about his "business trips," followed by why his clothes smell like perfume, followed by explaining the hotel charges on the credit card, and on and on.

4. *The sins of the Heart* are things harbored inwardly that are contrary to God's nature, such as greed, hate, revenge, or regret. Regret eats away at the soul. A mom regrets the last words to her son were angry and criticizing. Hatred leads to murder. The employee who hates his boss will look for the opportunity to either lash out verbally, physically or even go on a shooting spree.

5. *Sins of the Emotions* are hurt, anger or dishonor caught in old situations. Emotional sin usually stems from bad past experiences when you were shamed, insulted, or dishonored. When you choose not to let the emotion go, you will be caught in emotional sin.

Apologies are verbal expressions of sorrow. "God, I am sorry I lost my temper at my boss" is not repenting. God wants you to change your heart and behavior. Repenting is confessing to be forgiven, so behavioral changes will be possible. After repenting, you do not carry an accumulation of resentment and anger.

Asking for forgiveness also is not repenting. "Joe, please forgive me for throwing rocks at your car." Asking for forgiveness is asking the victim to do something while you, the perpetrator, do not necessarily change. Joe's forgiveness does not set the stage for your behavior to change. Sin will still stand in the mind and heart that holds bitterness, resentment, and unforgiveness.

So how do I repent? Repentance is taking responsibility for your actions and confessing sin before the Lord. True repentance involves your hand, head, and heart.

Your **hand** is what you did or failed to do. Only one-third of the job is done if you repent of the deed. The other two-thirds of the sin remaining will certainly cause your hand to err again.

The **head** plans the action. Planning can take five seconds or five years, so you must repent of the planning to do wrong.

The **heart** holds the anger, resentment, grudge, jealousy, or any other attitude that is not in alignment with God. That too, needs repentance for a complete break from the sin.

> **"Lord, I *repent* of throwing rocks at Joe's car (hand). I *repent* of planning to damage his property (head). I repent of holding anger, bitterness, and resentment in my heart against Joe because his dog barks at night (heart). I now *repent* and choose to receive your forgiveness. Amen."**

Unrepented sin will accumulate and derail your life. God promises to remove sin from your life when you repent.

He does not keep a score of repented sin.

If the same thing happens again, that new sin stands alone and repentance is needed. Once it is repented, it's gone. Repentance brings His righteousness.

When you repent, you come into alignment with God so He can reign in your life. When Jesus said, "Repent for the Kingdom of God is at hand," He calls you to freedom to make life changes in alignment with Him. This is the gift of realignment inside the Salvation package.

The Notebooks

There is no condemnation for those who are in Christ Jesus. (Romans 8:1)

This is a picture the Lord gave me to understand the power of repentance.

I was on a playground. The Lord was on one side of the field with a notebook writing down all the things I was doing. On the other side of the field, opposite Him, Satan was also with a notebook writing down all the things I was doing.

Satan was taking note of the good and bad things. He had plans to twist the good things and plans to build condemnation and accusations over bad things. He would say things like, "Got her now! You'll never get that straight. You blew it again. This is the 3rd time!" When I listened to Satan, the accusations and condemnations grew louder and so insistent that I began to believe them.

Meanwhile, the Lord was saying, "Watch out. You have stepped the wrong way. Come closer to me. Don't go that way. Bring those things over to me. Repent and Forgive."

When I repented, the Lord erased that item from his notebook. Amazingly, when it was erased from the Lord's notebook, the same offense noted in Satan's book vanished. There was nothing to condemn. When I brought the glory of the good things to the Lord, they too were removed from Satan's notebook so they could not be developed into prideful boastings.

We are all on the playground of life. We make mistakes and get on a track away from God. We take offense when others sin against us. Listen to the Lord today and hear his call to draw closer to him. Repent and forgive. You can empty Satan's notebook, so you do not have to live under his condemnation.

By Marcia Vogl, Reprint by permission christiandevotions.us.

Summary

The Gift of Salvation is something God prepared for you and all Mankind for a very long time. He knew you would be faced with many situations that would separate you from Him. His plan is a comprehensive one that is for good and not for evil. He wants to be your Savior, friend, and companion. These are the things He provides through Salvation.

1. Rescue: He pulls you out of bad situations.
2. Redemption: He gives you value.
3. Restitution: He makes up the difference in your loss.
4. Reconciliation: He brings you back into alignment for behavior change.
5. Repentance: Opportunity for sin to be forgiven.

CHAPTER 2

Salvation Tool Box

My grandson was so excited to receive the Christmas gift of a new motorized train. After we helped him put the cars together and set up the track, he discovered "batteries not included." What a disappointment! Fortunately, I was able to recharge his enthusiasm when I produced batteries.

Salvation is an ongoing journey with Jesus. He has done the initial part in rescuing you from sin and death. You can assemble the pieces to build something great from all you have been given. The Bible is your directions manual with me and other mentors guiding you. Get on the right track. Batteries are included! The following teachings and illustrations will show you how.

New Citizenship

But grow in the grace and knowledge of our Lord and Savior Jesus Christ. (2 Peter 3:18)

Growing is a process. Plants grow, animals grow, and people grow. All start as small, weak fledglings, but eventually, they get stronger and more mature. When you emerged from your mother's womb, you were born with flesh and blood and working body organs. You were not asked when or where you wanted to be born. You did not choose who you wanted for parents or what ethnic group you wanted to be. God decided all things according to his plan for you. At your physical birth, you were born as a "citizen into the Kingdom of the World."

At physical birth, you were gifted "free will. " However, your soul was like the soul of Adam *after* he and Eve ate from the restricted Tree of Knowledge of Good and Evil. Their disobedience brought death to the relationship with God, which got embedded in you. Because of Jesus Christ, you are given a choice to be born into the new life stream called "citizen of the Kingdom of God." You don't work for it. You don't wish for it. You don't make it happen. You intentionally *chose* it as a "spiritual birthright." That second trajectory is called "born again." In the world, the "born again" soul is the baby that needs to grow up spiritually. Water baptism is the sign of supernatural washing of your human spirit. Although your physical body does not change, your soul is put on a different trajectory with Jesus removing sin. With **Jesus as Savior,** you can implement the Scriptures as a lifestyle to connect with God.

Any part of your life that is out of control and not aligned with God needs a Savior. If your finances are in shambles, your relationships are broken, and your thinking is paranoiac, you need a Savior to straighten things out. If you make **Jesus as Savior** by lining up with His ways, things can get better. He will work on your finances, your relationships, and your mind. Permit Him to "Save" you.

When you accept **Jesus as Lord**, He can be Lord over those things in life you allow him to touch. If you disregard financial responsibility, relationship respect, and good health habits, He cannot be Lord over those things you choose to keep under your "old nature" of worldly living. It all comes down to your choice. He will not force you to accept his ways. He will woo you and encourage you instead.

God the Father gave all his creative power, restorative power, healing power, mercy, grace, and joy to Jesus. Jesus gives his followers everything He has received from the Father. Salvation gives you the same birthrights from God the Father that Jesus has. You are a son or daughter of the Kingdom of Heaven. These birthrights are not earned, worked for, or paid for. They are given to be used, cherished, and honored:

These are your birthrights.

1. You have **membership** in the Kingdom of Heaven.
2. You are **redeemed** by the Blood of Jesus and made Holy.
3. You have the **power** of the Blood of Jesus and the name of Jesus.
4. You have the **gifts** of the Holy Spirit.
5. You can walk in the **Perfect Will of God**.
6. You can **come boldly** before the throne of God.
7. You have **boundaries** to protect you.
8. You have **discernment** as a warning system.

Visitor, Resident, or Master

My eyes will watch over them for their good,
and I will bring them back to this land.
I will build them up and not tear them down;
I will plant them and not uproot them.

(Jeremiah 24:6)

We frequently invite people over for dinner. We love their company and enjoy hearing about their life adventures. After a three to four-hour dinner and **visit**, the guests leave. On special occasions such as family birthdays or Thanksgiving, people usually stay longer—maybe all day—but in any case, they eventually leave by nightfall.

When our son was a senior in high school, his buddy, who at age 18, had to leave his home because his parents were divorced and there was much turmoil in the home. We invited this young man to reside with us so he could at least graduate from high school before going out on his own. He became a **resident** in our home. We offered him a room of his own and meals. He had to abide by our rules and lifestyle—no alcohol, no drugs, and no obscene language allowed, and he must attend school regularly. He was a resident at our address.

My husband and I, as owners, are the **masters** of our home. We decide on the furnishings, what color to paint the rooms, and when, who, or what can come in. As masters over the house, we are also responsible for the repairs, cleaning, and activities.

Is Jesus a visitor, a resident, or a master in your life? When you just "invite" Jesus into your life, He is a guest for your enjoyment for a limited time then He leaves at your bidding. When Jesus is a resident, he lives in you but is still under your lifestyle choice. He can participate with you, but ultimately, you hold the keys. When you make Him Master over your life, you give him authority to make changes and you co-operate.

He can rearrange the furniture, decide what needs to be removed, how to keep things clean, and even decide who or what can come in. This requires a leap of trust.

Is Jesus Master of your life where he has permission to make changes in you?

Reprint "used by permission christiandevotions.us."

Recipe for Sanctification

*But just as he who called you is holy,
so be holy in all you do.*

(1 Peter 1:15)

When you receive Jesus as your Lord and Savior, you have gained the **ability** to make changes. It is NOT the change itself. You are in a *position* to receive the blessings of God. The question will be, "Are you in the *condition* to receive the blessings for your new life?"

You, as a marathon runner, will pay your entrance fee, suit up, put on your official racer number, and stand at the starting line to be in *position* for the marathon. If you have trained running, kept your body in good condition, and prepared your mind for this race, you will succeed. If you did not train, the chances are that you will not make it to the finish line because of fatigue, exhaustion, and perhaps a weak mindset. The Christian life is a marathon. You must be ready for the long haul. Sanctification is the process of preparing to run the race.

Cake Mix example

A box of cake mix has everything needed to become a cake except for the addition of water, oil, eggs, some mixing, and baking. If the mix is spread on the rose plants in the garden or put in a warehouse, it will not meet its destiny to be a lovely cake to delight people. Toxic substances or putrid ingredients in a cake would make it inedible. Therefore be careful to put only clean, wholesome ingredients in your life. Unholy ingredients like gossip, complaining, and self-pity will contaminate you. Do not look toward evil things like greed, lawlessness, or the occult to give you power. Evil will separate you from God.

You have everything needed inside you to fulfill your life's plan.

- Add *Water* which is the Word of God or the Scriptures.
- Add anointing *oil* that puts supernatural ability on your natural abilities.
- Be *yoked* (egg yolks) with Jesus so life will not be dry and crumbly.
- Mix all the ingredients at medium speed with *faith*. There is no high-speed fast track to faith-building.

You need to be *baked in the fire of the Holy Spirit* at the right temperature for a designated time. Doubling the heat for half the time does not work for cake baking.

Jumping into a swimming pool without knowing how to swim could spell disaster. You may not drown, but your swimming will be inefficient or become very tiring. The process of sanctification prepares you for the Christian life. Yes, a process! This does not happen instantly. Don't jump into the Christian life without preparation.

The process of sanctification moves you toward God and His plan for you. All is not lost if you make bad choices or mistakes along the way. You can repent getting back on track. You may have to take a scenic route, but you CAN get back on track. God is faithful. He is more ready and eager for you to fulfill your destiny than you are. His plans are for good and not for evil.

Citizenship Benefits

Jesus answered, "Very truly I tell you, no one can enter the kingdom of God unless they are born of water and the Spirit. Flesh gives birth to flesh, but the Spirit gives birth to spirit." (John 3:5)

In your "born again" life, the Holy Spirit is ready to replace the worldly spirit of self-sufficiency. Think of the gifts of the Holy Spirit like a Swiss army knife that has many tools in one compact implement. There is a knife, saw, screwdriver, and even scissors. You may not use all of these at the same time, but they are at your disposal depending on what you need.

The Upper Room was the scene of the Holy Spirit tongues of fire empowerment. (Acts 2:1-4) The disciples were empowered with boldness to speak in different languages and to preach Jesus to all those in attendance regardless of their backgrounds. These disciples did not first get degrees in Biblical studies or attend schools of ministry. Although today that is helpful, you too need Upper Room empowerment to be able to proclaim the Kingdom of God with power. With Holy Spirit empowerment, any education or training you have will be enhanced and you will be able to reach people of other languages and customs.

After I received the empowerment of the Holy Spirit, I could speak in tongues. I joined doctors in a once-a-month clinic for far-flung Mexican villages. Although I am not a medical professional, I could help by taking dictation from the doctors. After a full day of clinic work, the clinic leader told many waiting patients the clinic must close before sundown. They must return next month. Can you imagine being turned away after walking for days from your village?

I offered to pray for people before leaving. I prayed by the Holy Spirit in tongues. The people only spoke Spanish, and I only spoke

English. When I prayed in tongues, they understood what I prayed and some even conversed with me. They spoke in Spanish, and I spoke in tongues. I could not tell you the content of the conversation, but the look of joy on their faces and laughter in their children told me it was all good. Although I have since then embarked on ministry studies, I still minister in the Holy Spirit in tongues bringing powerful results.

Activation of the Holy Spirit allows you to use all the gifts and following powers available to you.

The Holy Spirit's **wisdom gifts** are the problem-solving gifts. These gifts empower you to use *wisdom, supernatural knowledge, and discernment* applied to situations to solve problems.

- There are times when God drops a "knowing" in your heart that you would not otherwise know. Late one night, I was awakened with a "knowing" that my daughter was in danger. I began to pray for her. She called to tell me the next morning she was falling asleep while driving back to college. She pulled over into a motel truck stop along the way to sleep. Although apprehensive, she was safely off the road and able to continue after a night's sleep. The "wisdom" was that she was in danger and needed prayer. Her concern was that I would question a motel bill on the credit card!
- Besides natural knowledge, God will give *supernatural knowledge* for breakthrough inventions, medical procedures, and strategies.
- The *discerning of spirits* is knowing right from wrong, the godly from the ungodly. Scientists who develop nuclear power must discern how to use it for good and not for evil.

The **vocal gifts** are supernatural communication gifts of *prophecy, tongues, and interpretation of tongues.*

- Prophecy is NOT fortune-telling. Prophecy is being able to say what God is saying. It can be an encouragement, a warning, or a forth-telling based on God's plan. Telling a young child he is

loved, encouraging a college student, and cautioning someone about life decisions are all prophecies.
- "Praying in the Spirit with tongues" is a *supernatural language* between you and God. It may sound like gibberish, but the Holy Spirit is in control of the communication. This takes getting your brain out of the way. As mentioned above, I prayed for my daughter in the Spirit since I did not know the situation. I could trust the Holy Spirit to direct my prayers. These prayers release a God-solution.
- The *interpretation of tongues* is given so that you and others can understand what is being said and share it with others. Sometimes the one praying gets the interpretation or another person in the group will interpret.

The **faith gifts** are *faith, miracles, and healing*. These gifts are announcements of who God is and what He will do for mankind.

- *Faith* is a gift that cannot be manufactured in your own strength or human reason. You choose to believe who God says He is and what He will do.
- You can expect God to do *miracles* when you ask by faith. I prayed with a friend, asking God for a miracle for her suicidal son. The next day her son related to her how he went into the woods with drugs with the intention of sleeping and never getting up. At dawn, he was awake and more alert than ever. He realized God's hand was upon him. God shows off his power in miracles.
- *Healing* is a gift to your physical body, mind, and spirit so that you can function as an empowered person. Do not be shy about praying for the healing of all kinds.

You have been given these Holy Spirit gifts to be successful in your second chance or "born again" state to live the life God planned for you. Getting goosebumps and punctuating every sentence with "Hallelujah" is not the proof of an activated Holy Spirit in the Christian. Although your exuberance may produce "Hallelujahs," the proof of a spirit-filled Christian is whether you function in the gifts of the Holy Spirit listed above. The evidence is in how you make decisions, how you speak, and how you behave.

Some people have a natural knack for sports, but with mentoring, training, and practice, they become superstars. Musicians, artists, teachers, mechanics, salesmen, and public speakers, all benefit from training that takes them to a higher level of competence.

Being able to function skillfully in the gifts of the Holy Spirit requires mentoring, training, and practice.

Fortunately, for you, the Holy Spirit provides that training by bringing others to teach you and speak to you directly if you agree to hear his voice and follow his directions.

To live as a mature Christian empowered to fulfill your destiny, you must walk with Jesus through maturity. It is not profitable to stay at the manger with the sweet baby Jesus. Do not stay at the cross and weep in distress. The journey passes through the tomb, to the upper room, and out into the streets where you live every day.

You can use all the gifts and powers available to you as found in 1 *Corinthians* 12:7-11: Invite Him to be activated in you today.

"Holy Spirit, I invite you to be activated in me."

Lessons from a BBQ

*They devoted themselves to the apostles' teaching
and fellowship, to the breaking of bread, and to prayer.
Everyone was filled with awe at the many wonders
and signs performed by the apostles.* (Acts 2:42-43)

Every Thanksgiving Day for about 20 years, I prepare the traditional turkey dinner for a large gathering of family and friends. I learned that roasting a turkey in a Weber BBQ takes about 3-4 hours, with no mess in the kitchen. Too many coals in at the beginning would just burn the edges of the food. Too few coals would leave the food undercooked or take much longer.

I fire up only 10 briquettes with my electric lighter. When they all are partially lit, I cluster them in a single layer in the middle of the briquette rack of the BBQ. Then I add a single layer of cold briquettes around the hot ones filling the briquette rack to the edge of the cauldron. By making sure the coals were touching another one, I ensured the lighted ones would ignite the cold ones, and those, in turn, would start the ones touching them. Eventually, the first ones would burn out, but the ones they lit would continue to light those in the outer ring. This method gave constant heat for at least two hours. After about two hours, I add ten more briquettes touching the ones already burning. The cooking heat can be prolonged by adding a few briquettes each hour until the food is cooked. I have done this many times, and each time, a beautifully BBQ roasted turkey is added to the table.

I realized this process can be duplicated for an "on fire" church. If you want to be on fire with the Lord, you need to gather with other people who want to be on fire too. Then find somebody or a few people who are already "on fire" and hang out with them. Pray with them. Study with them. Worship with them and fellowship with them. Even if you are not on fire YET, you will be ignited by touching their fire. Eventually, you will be "on fire" for the Lord and accomplish your purpose. You will ignite others to become "on fire" for the Lord in the process. Once you have fulfilled your destiny, you will turn into an ember, and the others will carry on.

The Power of Ask, Seek, and Knock

*"**Ask** and it will be given to you;*
***seek** and you will find;*
***knock** and the door will be opened to you."*

(Matthew 7:7)

When we brought home our 2 ½-year-old adopted daughter, she was non-verbal, or so we thought. She could follow directions like "stand up," "sit here," or "Do you want me to hold you?" But when she wanted something like water or a cookie, she sat silently with downcast eyes. The "20 questions" game worked to figure out what she wanted. There was nothing wrong with her speech abilities, and she knew the name of things like cookies or water. I realized I had to teach her how to ask. I started requiring her at least to attempt one word about what she wanted. After a few rounds of this, she learned that she had to ask. She soon also learned the proper protocols of "please" and "thank you."

Too many times, you fail to ask for something because you decided that "He is too busy," "He would not want to anyway," or "I don't deserve it." Even though the Lord knows what we need before we ask, He tells you to ask boldly of the Father regardless of circumstances.

To **ask** is to verbalize and clarify your request. I would like a new dress, or ice cream, or a car is much more definitive than "something." Speaking puts the power in your request. A relationship develops through asking. Although God knows what you need, He does not operate as a mind reader. When you ask, you are taking a position of submission and humility. You need to ask for *your* sake, not His.

Seeking is a process of purposefully being involved in activities that will bring about the desired result. Physical fitness requires exercise and not couch sitting while playing video games. Working out in a gym once a month will not bring the same results as workouts three to four times a week. If you seek healing, fill yourself with healing Scriptures, follow good health practices, and seek a doctor's advice. If you want financial prosperity, seek how to handle your money responsibly. Find out how God operates in prosperity.

To **knock** is not to be confused with wishful thinking. Get ready to lay hold of the prize. If you have been preparing for that perfect job, then take it when it's offered. Prepare your life for that special someone so when he/she appears, get connected. Don't sit on the side and wish.

Forgiving Yourself, Institutions, and God

"Do not judge, and you will not be judged.
Do not condemn, and you will not be condemned.
Forgive, and you will be forgiven."

(Luke 6:37)

As you learned in chapter 1, there is power in forgiving. You now know about breaking any link of sin by forgiving people who have hurt or sinned against you. However, the three entities that we frequently forget to forgive are ourselves, institutions, and God.

1. **Forgive yourself:** Holding a grudge against yourself is just as toxic as holding a grudge against another person. When you are plagued with thoughts of things you wish you had done or didn't do, you need to forgive yourself as if you were someone else. For example:

   - I wish I had called my mother more often.
   - If I had only finished college, things would be different.
   - If I had been quicker to see the signs of abuse, I could have …

The accusations against yourself run rampant. No one can stop them because they are self-produced. Regret and self-hate make you vulnerable to suicide, unexplained headaches, and debilitating health. Immune disorders, fibromyalgia, ulcers, or any disease that inhibits proper body functioning are sometimes signs of self-unforgiveness. Do not neglect being reconciled with yourself.

Not forgiving yourself is a subtle form of idolatry. If you believe God cannot or will not forgive you, you are making yourself greater than God. Repent for setting yourself up as greater than God.

Prayer for forgiving yourself:

> *"Lord, I forgive myself for (irresponsibility at the office, dishonoring my parents, not spending more time with my children). I do not owe myself anything: no restitution, no apology, no reasons, no explanations, and no excuses. I release myself 100%. John 20:23 says, 'If I forgive, I am forgiven. If I retain the sins, they are retained.' I now accept forgiveness from me. I repent for holding these things against myself."*

2. **Forgive institutions**: Forgive institutions such as the Department of Motor Vehicles, the university, or the police department. Because these do not have a face or a person you can identify, it does not mean you were not hurt. Because you were hurt, you need to forgive.

Unforgiveness will fester and sprout a harmful root of rage and violence. When people believe they have been treated unfairly by the police, they put the rage on any policemen or security officer in uniform. "Peaceful" marches go awry because there is no forgiveness. Remember, forgiveness does not mean the hurtful act is condoned. Forgiveness means you seek justice through God's intervention.

Prayer for forgiving institutions:

> *"Lord I forgive <u>(the hospital, insurance, university) for (losing my records, delaying my payments, making me do the work all over again)</u>. They owe me nothing—no restitution, no apology, no reasons, no explanations, and no excuses. I release them 100%. I look to you for justice in this situation. I repent of holding any revenge or resentment in my heart."*

3. **Forgive God**: Holding a grudge against God will cut off your relationship with Him. When he does not perform the way you wanted or expected, you perceive Him as having hurt you. Although the mind says, "God does no wrong," the heart says, "He has let me down." It is the heart that needs to forgive. Be specific.

I lost my first child in pregnancy due to rubella. I was angry at God because I believed he could have prevented the disease from affecting me, but He didn't. He let me down. I had to forgive him if I wanted Him to continue in my life going forward. You cannot be angry at God and still worship him in spirit and truth. There is a conflict between your emotions and your head, making you feel like a "push-me-pull-you." Platitudes such as "God meant for it to happen," "Keep being grateful for what you have," or "There is something to learn here," do not work! Forgive God! If you hold something against God, you are preventing your blessings from reaching you. He is waiting for you to confess and forgive so He can pour out his blessings.

Prayer for forgiving God:

"Lord, I forgive you for…(letting my child be molested, not curing cancer in my husband, letting our home be destroyed by the tornado, etc.) I forgive you for letting me down. I forgive you for not doing things the way I wanted them. I repent for holding a grudge against you. You do not owe me anything: no restitution, no apology, no reasons, no explanation, and no excuses. I release you 100%.
Amen

The Good, Acceptable and Perfect Will of God

Do not conform any longer to the pattern of this world, but be transformed by the renewing of your mind. Then you will be able to test (try out) and approve (see the goodness of) what God's will is—his Good, Pleasing, and Perfect will. (Romans 12:2-4)

An earthly Will is written so that survivors will know what to do with your estate after you die.

God's Will is written for you while you are living.

The Bible says, "God has a plan for you that is for good and not for evil." God's plan for you is called his Perfect Will. The key to knowing the Perfect Will of God is not "future telling." It is **obedience**. Living in the perfect will of God is fulfilling and joyful.

First, your thinking must be "renewed," not rearranged. When something is renewed, the old attachments are removed. When you renew your driver's license, the old information no longer applies. The date is new, the expiration date is new, the current address is new, and your photo is new. When your mind is renewed, the old way of thinking no longer applies.

Satan sets the pattern of this world with a "Me first" mentality so you will think and behave like him. "Do whatever it takes to get *my* way." The renewed mind thinks, "God first." Only when you no longer apply the "Me First" mindset can you see and operate in The Good, Acceptable, and Perfect Will of God.

The **Good Will** is what God bestows on everybody without prejudice.

The sun rises, the rain falls, and the crops grow for you whether or not you worship God. Gravity works on the prisoner, the pauper, and the privileged. We all benefit from God's goodness.

The **Pleasing Will** is within the boundaries God has set, such as the Ten Commandments, honoring God, and respecting others. Choosing to live according to God's standards brings benefits from the *Pleasing Will*. You stay in the *Pleasing Will* through repentance and forgiveness as the way to get back on track. When you live in The *Pleasing Will*, you can approach the throne of God without fear because you will have nothing to hide. You can be sure He hears you, and you will hear him. Blessings will flow to you and through you.

The **Perfect Will** is the particular assignment God has for YOU at a certain place, a certain time in history, and even a certain event. The *Perfect Will* is the place of fulfillment and joy. You may be a doctor to whom God will give the secrets to developing a cure for Parkinson's disease. If you choose not to do research, you will not be in His *perfect will*, and that destiny for you will not be fulfilled. You could still be a good doctor, but when you reject the *Perfect Will* for you, He will pass the privilege on to someone else.

God's *Perfect Will* develops in stages and requires perseverance. You may first work as a farmhand, learning how a farm is run. You study agriculture by observation and through technology. As you observe the farm and listen to God, He will give you ideas on how to produce better food sources. You can then help other farmers in countries struggling to feed their populations. In the whole process, you will be sharing the Kingdom of God.

I believe the "mom season" of my life was to be "the best mom for my children,"—**not** the "Best Mom in the World." That would be impossible and not God's *perfect will* for me. My job was to raise *my* children to be responsible adults in the Lord. As long as I was faithful to that calling during those years, I was in His *Perfect Will*. When my children became independent adults, His *perfect will* assignment changed to being a mentor to young moms raising their children.

In Summary:

1. You are in God's **Good Will** if you are living and breathing on this planet, where the sun rises, gravity works, and you don't have to do anything to make it happen.

2. You must choose to live in the **Pleasing Will** of God where His rules apply. Jesus constantly restores you to the Pleassing Will when you repent and forgive. This is grace and mercy in action, not performance.

3. You live in the **Perfect Will** when you are obedient and faithful to do your assignment. Whatever he ordains, he will sustain. He will give provision for the vision. This Perfect Will is tailor-made for you. The result is always for His glory.

Expectations and Boundaries as Your Shield

May it please you to prosper Zion, to build up the walls of Jerusalem. (Psalm 51:18)

Your prosperity should not be an open game for the world. When God created Adam, He put him in a garden to cultivate, watch over, and defend. This garden would prosper under God's guidance. God also gave you a "garden" or territory to cultivate, watch over and defend under His watchful eye. Both expectations and boundaries are needed to keep your garden defended and cultivated. Expectations are measures you set up for others.

Unmet expectations potentially plant negative seeds. You can expect others to be courteous, respectful, efficient, smiling, and even helpful. When they are not, you can become disappointed, angry, depressed, or even resentful. Do you go into a tizzy or a funk if your boyfriend does not send flowers for your birthday? Do you get angry when restaurant service is slow? In any case, it's always good to check your expectations.

1. Are they realistic? Can anyone be in two places at the same time? Do you expect people to never make mistakes or never fail? Whatever you expect of others will be expected of you.

2. Can your expectations be met or are you fantasizing? Expecting your dream man to come riding in on a white horse might be only a dream.

3. Are your expectations positive or negative? Expecting people to succeed or meet your needs is positive. But, if you think that the occasion will be a failure before it begins, you are negative. "The people at the party will ignore or annoy me" is a setup for a negative experience.

4. Is your way the only way? At times we think there is no other way to solve a problem. A woman who gained sobriety through Alcoholics Anonymous urged the other alcoholics she knew to join the program. She was surprised to learn some found fitness and athletics to be their exit.

The best antidote for unmet expectations is forgiveness. Forgive others for not meeting your expectations. Forgive yourself for putting unrealistic expectations on others or yourself. Harboring resentment, anger, or disappointment will only turn into bitterness. Bitterness brings death to your garden.

Jesus expected Peter, James, and John to stay awake and pray with him in the Garden of Gethsemane, but they could not. (Mark 14:32-42) He did not berate them. He continued on His assignment.

You must also set boundaries as safety measures to prevent others from overreaching. Jesus had boundaries. His priority was to preach in other towns, so he left when the people pressed him to stay to heal the sick (Luke 4:34-48).

1. Do you have a limit on how much time is spent on casual chit-chat? Too much chatter, gossiping, and mindless talk gobble up time and rob you of the opportunity to be productive.

2. Do you allow others to speak to you disrespectfully? Don't! Be firm, not belligerent, in stating you do not tolerate disrespect. If it is prudent, leave the scene, either physically or emotionally.

3. Can you say "no" politely without having to explain yourself? Sometimes you need to state a fact more than once. "I'm sorry I will not be able to attend" should be sufficient to decline an invitation even when pressed for an explanation.

Others will honor you if you honor yourself. Set up a few boundaries for yourself to keep self-respect and self-honor.

It is a pitfall to believe you have to accept any behavior from anyone as a measure of "love." To allow others to dishonor you is not a sign of love. Sometimes it is more loving to stop someone from sinning against you than to let them continue. If you don't want to go to the movies, decline rather than go anyway and hate yourself afterward. If you don't want to lend your car, clothing, or tools, don't lend them no matter how much someone begs. Do realize, though, that boundaries also have consequences.

1. If you do not allow anyone into your home or car, then don't be surprised if you feel isolated.
2. If you don't ever want to use public restrooms, then your travels will be limited.
3. If you only want to be among certain kinds of people, then your circle of friends will be limited.

Be mindful of not violating the boundaries of others. If someone does not want to go to a science fiction movie with you, respect them and don't ridicule them. If they turn down an invitation to a party without explanation, respect their decision and don't pester them. When telephone salespeople launch into pushing a product you do not want, do not be afraid to interrupt and politely say, "No, thank you, I am not interested," then end the call. There is no need to be rude, just firm.

If you are unhappy about your expectations or boundaries, re-evaluate them but don't give them up. They are important for order in your life. Remember, *expectations* are what you set up for others. *Boundaries* are what you set up for yourself.

Just as Jesus stayed on track for his purpose and destiny, you can too.

The Invisible and Visible Realms

For in him all things were created: things in heaven and on earth, visible and invisible, whether thrones or powers or rulers or authorities; all things have been created through him and for Him. (Colossians 1: 16)

There are two realms in existence at the same time. The natural, visible realm is what we see, such as our house, cars, money, children, jobs, etc. The invisible realm holds all the blessings God has for us waiting to manifest. He is waiting to release them to us at the right time. We have the privilege of being in a relationship with Him, so we need to ask for them. We are sons and daughters of the King of Kings.

Your grandparents know you, love you, and want the best for you. When you ask them for a new outfit, the chances of getting it are good because they want the best for you. Like your grandparent, God's love for you is so great that He will grant your request at the right time. He will not give a 10-year-old a car until he is able and capable of driving.

The invisible realm holds tangible and intangible things. The key to receiving favor is a pure heart. God looks upon the heart to see which ones are turned toward Him. If we ask, but our hearts are not turned toward God, and the intent is to use the gifts for our glory or mischief, he does not release it. You also need to know that the devil can give you what you want with malicious intent. Be sure you know who the giver is.

The desire for a spouse is to have a working covenant relationship that builds a godly family or a supportive love relationship. It's ok to ask for a handsome, rich dude or a glamourous intelligent woman. Just be sure your intent is correct. Do you just want the money, the prestige, and the outward visage of a power couple? Do you want a woman to be an arm trophy or one you can respect and be proud of? You can express your desire for a spouse. You both need to be prepared for your life together that reflects God. Know what kind of person you are and what would complement you. Many couples have found the love of their life and have had many happy years of marriage. Marriage is a covenant relationship meant to last a lifetime, not only until you get tired.

Jobs hang in the invisible realm for you if you are willing to pull them down from heaven. Linda was praying for a new job. She told me how tired she was with her current job. Although the work was interesting, she didn't like the people. She complained about the pay and judged the boss and co-workers. After we prayed, I advised her to repent and get rid of her bad attitude. God looks upon the heart, not just your expertise. After she repented of her disgruntled attitude and forgave those around her for what she saw as flaws, she felt a lifting of her spirit and was refreshed. Within a week, she was contacted by an agent with a new job offer in her line of work with better pay, benefits, and location.

Sherry had a very high-level position in her industry. She wanted to move closer to home as the commute was taxing on her and robbed her of many hours with her family. She prayed and asked the Lord for her "perfect" job. She waited in faith, but nothing happened. She made sure her heart was clean before the Lord. Doing due diligence, she applied for openings and went on several interviews waiting for a door to open. As our group prayed, someone said, "Don't look for a door. Pull it down from heaven!" We redirected our prayers, and she pulled from the invisible realm her new job into the natural realm. The next day, she called us to say the perfect job offer came to her.

The servant of Elisha feared the natural army coming after Elisha. "Don't be afraid," the prophet answered. "Those who are with us are more than those who are with them" (2 Kings 6:16). We can have the same vision in our situations.

We can also pull out of the invisible realm peace, joy, confidence, solutions, wisdom, and whatever we need at the time. Make sure your heart is clean before the Lord. Remove any ulterior motives and any sin on your hands. Usually, the Lord has gifts greater than we can desire or pray for.

When my eldest child was entering college, I sought a job to help pay for college tuition. I formerly had been a music teacher in elementary & junior high school and a college instructor. But that was 15 years earlier. Getting back into the work world was daunting. The music teaching world had changed, and I wasn't sure I could catch up. I asked the Lord for a job that would be 8 to 5 with no homework. I just wanted to leave it at the end of the day. I was assigned to a mortgage company through a temporary work agency to do minimal typing. That was clearly below my ability as one with two college degrees with a 90-word-per-minute typing speed. I accepted it as a start. I set out to be the best typist, the best copy machine girl, and the best all-around "go-fer." After 6 weeks, the company offered to hire me. They were surprised I had two college degrees and teaching experience. I was offered relatively low pay, but since I was only working for college tuition for my son and wanted set hours, I accepted the job. The Lord blessed me with favor as I learned the industry well enough to be promoted to supervisor of the documentation department. I was not laid off when the industry dropped, and I received maximum raises and bonuses. I also worked with wonderful people and ministered informally during my twelve years there. When I was finally laid off because of company "restructuring," I received maximum severance pay and bonuses. I learned the mortgage industry well enough to structure my own property ownership as an extra advantage.

I thought I was always going to be a music teacher. I am still a teacher, but now I have the best opportunity to give God glory through teaching about His Kingdom through my books and ministry. This "job" was delivered and developed from the invisible realm.

CHAPTER 3

The Blessing Thief

In Genesis 3, Satan is referred to as the Serpent that originally lured Mankind into sin. His goal is to supplant God. He opposes anyone who desires to live in obedience to God. The Christian is his nemesis.

Satan is a Deceiver who uses trickery to keep you and all Mankind from living under God's reign to deprive you of heaven's blessings. He schemes to kill, steal, and destroy all that God loves, including you. Be wise in avoiding his traps and be aware of his tactics. Should you stumble, you will know how to get up to fight back. The following section lets you see what is behind the veil of deception.

Who is Satan?

*"I will ascend above the tops of the clouds;
I will make myself like the Most High."*

(Isaiah 14:14)

Satan is NOT a figment of the imagination, a literary figure, or a harmless spirit. He would like you to think that so you will not pay attention to his schemes.

Satan (also referred to as The Devil) was created by God to be the Archangel, leading worship in heaven. He was beautiful, and his body was of pipes that vibrated with majestic music. He made awesome worship music. However, he wanted to supplant God and believed he could be equally powerful and wonderful as God. To fulfill his lust for power, Satan convinced one-third of the angels to follow him in a rebellion. Consequently, God banished him and his rebel angel entourage from heaven. Those banished angels are now demons and minions on earth. You can find all this in the book of Isaiah in the Bible.

Mankind was created to worship God, praise, and adore Him with song, dance, and a pure lifestyle. God, the Creator of the Universe, gave **Adam** (Mankind) dominion over the earth as the chief worshipper. Satan hates being replaced by Mankind; therefore, he is against all people. Satan hijacked Adam's dominion over the earth by luring Eve to eat of the Tree of Knowledge of Good and Evil. She then invited Adam to disobey God, thus joining the rebel company. This disobedience resulted in Mankind's separation from God, called *death*.

Satan's goal is to lure Mankind out of alignment with God through disobedience. When you worship anyone or anything other than God, Satan gains the power to corrupt the earth and its people. He is a liar, deceiver, killer, thief, and destroyer. He can only destroy but cannot create. He brings death, not life. He is everything God is not.

Satan will use anyone to rouse your anger against God by speaking to you through your mom, dad, friends, spouse, and even your children. This does not mean these people are evil. Often they are unaware of how they are being manipulated by Satan to hurt you. It can be through criticism, foul language, slurs, judgments, and even "jokes." If you are unaware of this tactic, you will either retaliate or nurse the hurts. When either happens, you are trapped.

Satan will use sickness to oppress you. Your body is key to bringing glory to God. When you are plagued with headaches, stomach pain, muscle aches, and poor eyesight, it is easy to focus on those things rather than God. Instead of seeking God for healing, the tendency is to blame God for the discomforts or disabilities.

Satan can manipulate you with money through poverty or wealth. Watch out for false prosperity through gambling, crime, or greed. Money can be a trap for worldly pleasures that degrades you or others. Lawful prosperity is God's plan. Academic learning, trade development, crafting, or inventions can move you out of poverty into prosperity.

Satan will put physical, mental, or emotional abuse on you so that you will blame God for your plight. God does not want to abuse you. He will work out ways for you to be a strong overcomer. I remember the story of a scientist who, after years of success, thanked the elementary school bully for chasing him after school every day. Knowing he could find safety in the library, he escaped there and read as many books as possible, showing the librarian he was not loitering. The situation introduced him to science, art, and literature. As an adult, no longer escaping a school bully, his appetite for learning of all kinds was whetted for an enriched life. He became a multifaceted educated man.

Satan will also use fame, money, or status to divert your focus away from God. Many rich have ruined their lives by choosing drugs, alcohol, and sexual crime because money gave them access. It might have been fun at the time, but addictions are prisons. From the outside, it may look like a "wonderful life," but in the soul, it's dark and full of death.

Satan does not play fair! He will do whatever it takes to steal you from God.

This is War!!! God holds the winning hand.

Spiritual Warfare

Be alert and of sober mind. Your enemy the devil prowls around like a roaring lion looking for someone to devour.

(1 Peter 5:8)

Satan comes to kill, steal, and destroy life. Jesus came to give life. You can conclusively say they are enemies.

God, the Creator, is greater than Satan! This is not an equal battle. God loves you. He has been working on your behalf for eternity. Satan has been working against you for a very long time. He hates it when you follow God and will try to lure you away. God is for you. Satan is against you. You need to decide which side you want to be on and how you are going to stay there.

**THE WAR IS NOT AGAINST YOU.
THE WAR IS OVER YOU.
YOU ARE THE PRIZE!**

Sometimes you might wish your enemy would "just go away." According to the Bible, that is not going to ever happen. The enemy must be defeated. You must know how to face your enemy if you are seeking to live life to the fullest with God.

When you belong to God, His enemies are your enemies. Lawlessness is in opposition to the God of Law and Order. Anything that does not honor the sanctity of life, such as murder, abuse, and innocent bloodshed, opposes the God of Life. Miscarried justice and prejudice of any kind defies the character of The God of Justice. Anti-Bible, anti-prayer, banning God in the public arena defies the God of Truth.

Hate movements with threats and ostracism are enemies of the God of Love. You become an enemy to yourself with behaviors, thoughts, and intentions that oppose God.

Fortunately, God has the winning strategy. **God gave Jesus Christ on the cross to break the bondage of any sin, no matter what it is.** This is Salvation in action.

To repent and forgive are key weapons in this warfare. Salvation with no repentance and forgiveness is like a gun with no ammunition. Your human-based path out of the world's influence of sin is powerless. You cannot work your way out of sin. You cannot reason your way out of sin. You cannot be kind enough or even give enough money to get out of sin. Sin is an alignment issue with the Word of God. Repentance and forgiveness align you with God.

Satan's Schemes

Then Jesus was led by the Spirit into the wilderness to be tempted by the devil. (Matthew 4:1)

Satan is so brazen that he tried to trick Jesus while He was on a 40-day wilderness retreat. Satan will use these same tricks on you. He waited until the 40 days were completed when Jesus would have been the weakest physically.

Trap #1: "First, make these stones into bread!"

Satan knew Jesus was hungry. Jesus said, 'I don't live by my bodily needs, but by the Word of God.' (Marcia's translation.) Satan will use your body to distract you. He will get you to either overeat or starve yourself. Then he will bring injury or sickness to make you so focused on your body that you lose sight of God. Jesus' battle was, "I do not obey my body. I obey the Word of God." That does not mean you don't listen to your body and take care of it. It means you don't let your bodily needs throw you off track from focusing on God.

Trap #2: "Jump down from the cliff and make God rescue you. He said he will!"

Satan will goad with "I dare you" statements. Jesus said, "Don't test God." In other words, don't do something stupid just to see if God will rescue you. God is your shield and protector when you are in danger but don't jump off buildings or bridges just to see if He comes to your rescue. Don't eat poison to see if He cures you. God will keep his promise when you need rescuing but do not deliberately put yourself in danger. You will be disappointed! God does not use his power to play games.

Trap #3: Satan said, "Worship me and I will give you all the kingdoms of the earth."

Adam and Eve disobeyed God when they listened to Satan. They, in essence, gave away their dominion over the earth. Satan knew Jesus' purpose on earth was to win back the earth to Mankind, so he was offering Jesus the easy way—worship Satan. What a deception! Jesus knew this would make him subject to Satan! Jesus told him, "I only worship God."

Satan still uses these traps today. He will say you can get what you want if you do things his way rather than God's way. "These drugs will make you feel good," "You can be rich if you embezzle the money," or "You can be famous." Sometimes God's way is more difficult. However, if you bow down to Satan, he will keep you in bondage. Satan is not the "nice guy" he would have you to believe. He will try to wring out every ounce of life in you.

The three main schemes of Satan are:

1. He will focus on your physical comforts and needs.
2. He will goad you to make God prove himself in manufactured situations. That is called "testing" God.
3. He will trick you into worshiping him with tantalizing offers.

Be aware and have your antennae up.

Stay in the shelter of the Lord. (Psalm 91)

WARNING: Do *NOT* Touch!

Eve said to Satan, "God did say, 'You must not eat fruit from the tree that is in the middle of the garden, and you must not touch it, or you will die." (Genesis 3:3)

Don't even touch it! God knows that is just the beginning of a downfall. Satan will convince you a little touch won't harm!

The lures of Satan are very subtle.

First, he lured Eve to "just look" at the tree. How harmful can "looking" be? Then she touched the fruit even though God told them not to touch it.

Making contact with sin will increase your desire for it. Satan will convince you that you can disengage whenever you want to. This is why a salesman urges you to touch the soft velvet couch or open the doors of the car and smell the new upholstery, or even kick the tires. Touching makes your desire greater. Eve then took the plunge and ate the fruit, even when she knew this was forbidden.

Of course, you want it. "Buy it!"

Next, she did not only keep the fruit for herself. She shared it with Adam sharing her sin. "Take the couch (car) home. Show your husband what a great buy it is!"

Remember the instructions of the Lord. "You must not touch it, or you will die."

1. Temptations: Don't *look* at what you were told not to touch.
2. Entertainment: Do not *consider* its possibilities.

3. Decision: Do not *rationalize* the consequences.
4. Don't *share* it with others.

You are given the choice to either heed God's warnings or listen to Satan's temptations. The wages of sin is death. You may not physically die, but your ability to remain holy and pure dies. DO NOT TOUCH.

Guilt vs. Shame

Therefore, there is now no condemnation for those who are in Christ Jesus. (Romans 8:1)

Frequently the words guilt and shame are used interchangeably, but they do not mean the same thing.

Guilt is acknowledging that you have done something improper, morally wrong, or out of alignment with God. There is evidence of your behavior. It carries the realization that someone else has been hurt because of your actions. Emotional remorse might lead you to admit the wrongdoing. Guilt can be anything from murder to slamming the door and waking up the baby.

Shame is a feeling of humiliation, regret, and distress on how you see yourself according to what you have done or someone did to you. Shame is a cloak that covers your personhood. A person who has been molested feels shame because she/he feels dirty, unclean, or violated. Shame shuts you down so that you cannot face or admit such a thing has happened.

Shame can be self-condemning too, according to your actions. You feel shame because you forgot your lines in the play, stumbled in the middle of the dance floor, or were the center of unwanted negative attention. Anything that makes you believe you are less than a valuable human being is shame.

The Bible says that Jesus has come to take away guilt and shame. How does that happen? Guilt can be washed away by repentance. Shame can be washed away by forgiving. Both are the benefits of the Blood of Jesus.

When you confess your sin or admit that you are out of alignment with God, you are forgiven by God. You are forgiven for whatever you confess or repent. You may be forgiven for each offense, but the Lord is waiting for you to change your behavior that hurts others. Until you repent, you will not be able to access grace to change. **It is through repentance that guilt is washed away.**

When you forgive others, you relinquish all rights to hang on to the hurt and pain. The tie of sin between the offender and the victim is removed, so shame cannot cover your soul. You must forgive yourself too, so you do not keep accusing yourself. If you forgot your lines or tripped on the dance floor, you need to forgive yourself so you can relinquish the right to self-accuse. If someone has put shame upon you, you need to relinquish the right to accuse him. **It is through forgiving others that shame is washed away.**

Prison Break

But the Lord has become my fortress, and my God the rock in whom I take refuge. (Psalm 94:22)

God is a stronghold for you. There is a moral wall around you that gives you freedom and protection as you go about life. Satan also wants to build a stronghold around you that imprisons you, restricting you from living fully. Sin breaks down God's moral wall. Satan gains entrance into your life. The root of all evil strongholds is sin—either committed by you or committed against you.

Once Satan enters your life through sin, he builds a stronghold protecting that gateway with evidence that supports the lies you believe. As long as you operate under his lies, he has open access to you. Satan sets strongholds in your life to keep you separated from God and from walking in God's plan for your destiny. You cannot get out by your own devices. No amount of behaviors, pleas, or exercises can free you. Only the Blood of Jesus, through repentance and forgiveness, will set you free so you can stay free.

How to identify a Stronghold:

- If you are confronted with sin and can easily repent, no stronghold can be built.
- If you justify sin and/or continue in it, you have built a stronghold.

Common justifications for strongholds:

- "Everybody does it." Righteousness is not determined by the number of subscribers.
- "That's just how I am." Sin is a choice.
- "It's acceptable today." God's righteousness never changes.

- "My whole family is like that." Past generational sins do not determine your future.
- "I'm not serious. Just joking." Don't joke with sin. Satan plays for keeps.
- "I couldn't help it. It just happened." Repent for the Kingdom is here.

Common grounds for strongholds:

- *Past Hurt Prison.* The accumulation of unreconciled past hurts will build a fortress. Each old wound increases in intensity until it is unbearable. If parents and teachers raised their voices at you, whenever a voice is raised, you squirm and feel attacked. It could be a preacher or a football coach. That stronghold can only come down when you *forgive* those who hurt you with their raised voices. You will be free from the old hurts and do not have to feel attacked.
- *Injustice Prison.* If you have been falsely accused, the pain of injustice lingers until you become belligerent to fend off future injustice, real or unreal. If you were frequently punished for a sibling's misdeed, the pain of injustice would return whenever you hear in the news about something you believe to be unjust. You will develop either a strong defense system or a mentality of helplessness. Whenever something does not go your way, you will see it as an injustice rather than an unmet expectation. There is no joy in the "injustice prison."
- *False Facts Prison.* As a woman, if you believe all men are only interested in sex, you will build a stronghold against men in general. You will not be able to build a good relationship with men as co-workers or friends. Your desire to date or be married will be thwarted. As a man, if you believe men should never cry, you will not be able to express tender emotions and only exhibit harsh emotions. The false facts will imprison you.

- *Your Judgment Prison.* Prisons are built by collecting evidence to support your judgments. Judging "all rich people are greedy" will prevent you from befriending rich people or becoming rich yourself for fear of being greedy. You may miss good opportunities because of the judgment stronghold. If you judge others as being selfish, argumentative, or ridiculous, those judgments will come back as a stronghold.

Here is a **pattern** for finding and breaking strongholds in all areas of your life. When you constantly meet roadblocks, admit there is bad fruit coming from a bad tree somewhere in your life. To be set free, you must find it and remove it.

1. *What is the fruit?*
   ("I frequently use sarcastic remarks" to convey mocking or contempt.)
2. *What is the root?*
   (When I feel threatened and helpless, I believe I have to strike with words.)
3. *Repent or confess the sin.* (I confess and repent of striking others with sarcasm.)
4. *Forgive those who sinned against you in the same way.* (I forgive those who have hurt me with sarcastic remarks.)
5. *Renounce and Break the bondage.*
   (I renounce sarcasm and break its hold over me. I release all hurts of sarcasm that were put upon me in the past. I shake them off.)
6. *Bless. Replace the lie with the truth of the Word.* (I will let my words be "yes" or "no". I will keep my tongue from speaking evil to remain in the presence of the Lord.)

From this example, insert any bad fruit you want to eliminate from your life. Usually, the bad fruit hurts either you or others.

1. What is the bad fruit?
   _____

2. What is the root? What is my greatest memory when this fruit came up?
   _____

3. What sin do I need to repent? _____
   _____

   "I repent of _____
   _____

   Who or what do I need to forgive? I forgive "_____
   for _____"

   "I forgive _____ for _____
   _____. They do not have to give me restitution, an apology, a reason, an explanation or an excuse. I release them 100%."

4. What is this stronghold called? _____
   _____

   "I renounce _____ and break its hold on my life."

5. What is God's truth that will replace the stronghold lie? "There is no condemnation for those who are in Christ Jesus. Through repentance and forgiveness, I am in Christ Jesus, therefore I am free of this stronghold." (1 Corinthians 8:1)

Remember, the key to repenting and forgiving is the power of the Blood of Jesus to remove the stronghold. Nothing else will work. When you have torn down the Enemy's prison, you then will reestablish God's stronghold in your life.

Self Entrapment: The Inner Vow

*I will fulfill the vows my lips promised
and my mouth spoke when I was in trouble.*

(Psalm 66:14)

**The devil's tactic is to get you to do
his dirty work.**

Yes, that could be you or me. When he can get you to set your own traps, he only has to sit back and watch you squirm. The kind of trap particularly sneaky is trapping yourself with inner statements that are in agreement with the devil and contrary to the word of God. Vows are very strong statements that should not be made lightly.

When things happen to you, you make inner statements without knowing you are doing it. The inner statement will either draw into what you have decided or will repel things that are contrary to it.

When in high school, I was always the last to be chosen on the physical education teams. I was not particularly athletic and stood only 4' 10." My inner statement said, "I am always the last one chosen." Although it was a fact in the physical education class, it showed up in other parts of my life. I was chosen to be on the homecoming court *after* the dance. I came in last in the student body election for treasurer. I became the assistant director of the Choraleers because no one else knew how to direct a chorus. I was chosen to be a speaker at a retreat because the one first chosen had to drop out. At first, I consoled myself with being a "pinch hitter." This inner statement had to be broken as the Bible says, "I am the head and not the tail."

The magnetic field I had set up was to "always be the last." This statement kept me from being grateful whenever I was first. In high school, I was editor-in-chief of the school yearbook, I was the school organist, and I was the president of the statewide Episcopal Young Churchmen. Somehow these "firsts" were hidden from me. I could not be grateful and enjoy those honors.

This statement trapped me from being who I was supposed to be. The Lord set me free when I repented of making the inner vow and coming into agreement with the lie. I forgave myself for setting my own trap. Today I can be either first or last accepting where the Lord puts me.

The inner statement of "I must be first or nothing" drives some people to be first in everything to the point of obsession. They become depressed and dissatisfied if they did not get a promotion, did not win the scholarship or are not chosen for the internship. Then, some hang back to make sure they will "always be the last." These avoid recognition for something good or may even sabotage their success to fulfill their inner statement of always being last.

Repent of agreeing with any statement the devil used to make you trap yourself. Break those inner statements. You can be joyful where the Lord puts you. You will be the head and not the tail, above and not beneath.

What "promise" have you made to yourself that is keeping you from prospering? "I'll always be poor," "Having money is bad," "I can't get what I want." Any of these will limit you. You find yourself doing anything to keep the vow, including sabotaging others and yourself.

Prayer to break inner vows:

Lord I repent of agreeing with the lie of the enemy that says: _____. I forgive myself for living that inner vow. Thank you for forgiving me. I now renounce that statement and no longer give it power in my life. I declare you are Lord over me.

The Art of Holy War

Therefore each of you must put off falsehood and speak truthfully to your neighbor, for we are all members of one body. (Ephesians 4:25)

We are not left to do battle with Satan and his demons without weapons and skills. The Blood of Jesus removes sin with repentance and forgiveness. The Word of God (Bible) is our sword which we must learn to use skillfully. (No Bible-bashing allowed.) The Bible defines who you are and who you are not. (Ephesians 1) The Bible tells who God is—Healer, Provider, King of Kings, the Almighty, the Great I AM.

Here are bullet points that reiterate how to enter the battle.

1. Cleanse your heart, mind, and body.
    a. Repent of agreeing with the lies of the devil.
    b. Repent of raising anything above God. Job, health, children, spouse, and parents can be idols.
    c. Repent of making ungodly packs with yourself. (Inner vow)
    d. Repent of holding anything in your heart contrary to God's character.
    e. Repent of anger, resentment, judgment, unforgiveness, bitterness, (ARJUB) See chapter 1.

2. Forgive completely (RAREEx): No Restitution, apology, reason, explanation, excuses.
    a. Forgive those who hurt you, lied to you, cheated you, etc.
    b. Forgive yourself for making ungodly agreements.
    c. Forgive institutions.
    d. Forgive God.

Break off Bondages after you have repented and forgiven.

3. Declare the agreements with lies are broken.
    a. "I declare the agreement I made that "I am clumsy" is now broken."
4. Break the curses that were brought on by sin. "I break the curse of poverty now that I have repented of giving bad checks."
5. Dissolve assignments that keep you from moving forward.
    a. Confess the trauma. *"I admit I was bullied in school."*
    b. Repent of wrong things in your heart. *"I repent of holding in my heart anger and resentment against those bullies."*
    c. Choose to forgive by faith. *"I choose to forgive them."*
    d. Break the assignment with the Blood of Jesus. *"The Blood of Jesus now dissolves the power of the past trauma that holds me in fear."*

Here are some points to remember when facing your enemy.

> **Step 1:** *Worship God in all circumstances.* (2 Kings 17:39)
> **Step 2:** *Live a lifestyle of holiness and righteousness.* (Ecclesiastes 2:26)
> **Step 3:** *You are empowered to dominate over your enemies.* (Romans 16:19)
> **Step 4:** *God will give you strategy and unusual plans.*
> **Step 5:** *Destroy the enemy's ability to rise again.*

Worship, holiness, and submission to God will enable you to have strategies and power to be victorious. You will have authority over your enemies after they have been delivered into your hands. These are foundational steps laid out for you in these pages.

**Keep focused on the ultimate goal:
WORSHIP GOD.**

The Lord at Your Side in Battle

The Lord will fight for you; you need only to be still.

(Exodus 14:14)

We are often reminded that he declared, "The battle is the Lord's." Does that mean we can sit back and watch the scenery with no responsibility? This battle cry is to let the Enemy know whose side we are on. There are three occasions in scripture that give us insight.

(Exodus 14:14) When Moses was leading the Israelites out of Egypt, they found themselves with the Red Sea in front and the Egyptian army at the rear. They were trapped. "The Lord will fight for you. You need only to be still." In this case, they had to stand back and let the Lord open the Red Sea, but they had to be ready to move forward through it. When you are between a rock and a hard place, wait and watch the Lord move on your behalf but don't get comfortable. Get ready to move out of that place.

(II Chronicles 20:1-21) When Jehoshaphat was faced with insurmountable odds in meeting the vast armies of Ammon and Moab, he was told, "The battle is not yours, but God's." He still had to organize his forces to advance and face the enemy, not to fight but to collect the spoils. They proceeded with praise. The weapon was praise to the Lord. When you are being challenged, praise the Lord ahead of time for the spoils you will gather.

(I Samuel 17:1-54) When David faced Goliath, he declared, "the battle is the Lord's," not by conventional means. David, however, had to use the slingshot skill he developed as a shepherd. He also went after Goliath in the name of the Lord without fear. He knew that with the Lord, there is guaranteed success. The rest of the Israelite army had to be ready to move out against the Philistines. When you are being threatened, know that your natural skills will be used supernaturally.

Three things to remember:

1. When you are trapped, be still but don't get comfortable. Get ready to move out.
2. When you are challenged, start praising and get ready to bring in the spoils.
3. When you are threatened, know the Lord will supernaturally use your natural skills.

Maxine told me how she was trapped in a lawsuit over the sale of her home. The tenant/buyers of one year accused her of contaminating the home as a meth lab. They had the home red-tagged as uninhabitable. All this was not true. The insurance company refused to insure the house, and she now had a four-bedroom renovated white elephant on her hands. We prayed in agreement that the Lord would send her an advocate and get her out of this situation. A week later, an attorney from the insurance company told her he was assigned to represent her in this false claim so her house could be recovered. The insurance company agreed to bear all litigation costs. She cooperated fully in providing documents. After two months of litigation, tests, and inspections, the house was cleared and made available to be put on the market for sale with no restrictions. She managed to sell the house at a fair market price. She learned to stand still yet ready to move with the Lord on her side.

CHAPTER 4

Wolves in Sheep's Clothing

*Then the **wolf** attacks the flock
and scatters it.* (John 10:12)

Not everything is as it seems. Christians can be deceived. There is nothing magical about becoming a Christian. You may feel different. Your thinking may change. Nonetheless, you must learn to discern the real from the fake, authentic from the copy. Fake does not advertise itself as a fake. It advertises as real. Many "knock-off" products look like designer goods. While shopping overseas, I found a name-brand jacket that looked, felt like, and seemed to be made like the "real thing" for a cheaper price. When I brought it home for my son, I learned from a friend that the big giveaway was that the logo should have been white and not light blue. The garment faded after being washed a few times, and the zipper broke easily. Because I did not know the details of the authentic item, I was deceived. Fortunately, this was not a life-threatening issue, and only little money was involved. I learned that the details count.

Wolves dressed in sheep clothing infiltrate the flock to deceive them into thinking they are one of them. The unsuspecting sheep can end up as a wolf's dinner. The scenarios in this section call your attention to deceptions that look good but are not good for you. Do not walk in fear. Fear will paralyze you. You are called to sharpen your seeing.

Stand in Your Faith

If you do not stand in your faith, you will not stand at all.

(Isaiah 7:9b)

In this Bible account, King Rezin of Aram and Pekah, king of Israel, tried to overpower Jerusalem when Ahaz was King of Judah. Although Ahaz survived this onslaught, he heard of future alliances against him. He was shaken. The prophet Isaiah came to tell him that such a future alliance against him would not succeed. The Lord gave Ahaz the long view—within 65 years—this proposed alliance would be stubble and worthless. "If you do not stand in your faith, you will not stand at all." was Isaiah's admonition.

Standing in faith is a long-term proposition that takes stamina, patience, and continual obedience. When faced with a challenge, we cannot stand on what we hear, what we see, or even what we know about the circumstances. Standing in faith is standing on what you know from God and about God.

God says He will meet your challenges. He will deliver you from evil—addictions, sickness, disease, and threats. He will provide for your needs—finances, security, affection, and education.

Assess what you believe. If there are any beliefs contrary to the Word of God, repent of agreeing with it. Sometimes the devil will give you the short-sighted version of God's truth. When you are healed through treatment, surgery, or rehabilitation, Jesus is still your Healer. If the healing takes time rather instantly, the devil will lead you to believe God is failing and will not come through for you. *Positive repentance* means to repent of believing the lie so you can take up God's truth as found in the Scripture. This removes lies and builds your faith.

Example of positive repentance:

"I repent of believing the lie that I am now useless due to this illness. I believe God has a plan for me, for good and not for evil. I am still valuable to Him regardless of the condition I am in. He loves me."

It's easier to repent of wrong beliefs than to repent of what you are NOT believing. *Negative repentance* leaves a void where more lies can come in. *Example of negative repentance:*

"I repent for *not* believing you have a plan for me."

This does not build a faith you can stand on. You must stand on the Word of God. If you come to a precipice in life, stand in faith that God is not going to push you over the cliff. He is the God of the impossible. He will either build a bridge, sprout wings on you or turn you around on another path. Keep standing until the miracle happens. Don't give up.

The Slippery Slope

My people, hear my teaching;
listen to the words of my mouth.

(Psalm 78:1)

Sometimes people find themselves out in the cold in their relationship with God. How did this happen? If you used to have a good relationship with God, can you recover? Psalm 78 will give you some insight into the slippery slopes of faith.

1. **You refuse to live by God's covenant and laws.** (Psalm 78:9) When you start to bend the rules and make excuses for your actions that are not in alignment with God's standards, the downhill fall begins. When you become so set in your reasoning and perspective, you forget what God has done for you—his blessings, wonders, his mercy, and kindness.

2. **You begin depending on your understanding.** (Psalm 78:19) Here, rebellion sets in your heart because you believe you know better than God. You start demanding things from Him because you want it a certain way. Although God promises provision, you want it in a check. He promises to heal, but you won't go to the doctor. He promises protection, but you make risky choices of danger.

3. **You are brought down low because of arrogance.** (Psalm 78:36) Because of rebellion and refusal to live according to his design, you fall to depths of hardship. Unfortunately, rather than repenting, you begin flattering God and thinking that saying the right things to him is going to rectify the situation. This is phony loyalty.

4. In this state, **you continue to harass God with petty things.** (Psalm 78:41) You accuse him of not answering prayer, not rescuing you, being far away, and even abandoning you.

5. **Your heart turns to idolatry.** (Psalm 78:58) When you abandon God, you begin to worship other gods or make things into gods. As long as you are worshipping another god of any kind, you will not be able to fulfill your destiny. **Unless you repent,** God will have to choose someone else to carry the standard and reap the blessings of your destiny so his will can be done.

Fortunately, you can repent at any stage of the fall and be restored to your destiny and the blessings that go with it. If you see yourself in any stage of sliding downhill, repent today and let the Lord restore you.

Come Out From Under the Shadow

The Lord is slow to anger, abounding in love and forgiving sin and rebellion. Yet he does not leave the guilty unpunished; he punishes the children for the sin of the parents to the third and fourth generation.

(Numbers 14:18)

All of us are born under the shadow of our ancestors. The sins of the fathers are visited upon the children in the third and fourth generations. The Word tells us this not to condemn us but to give us revelation on where to find the root of the problems. Unrepented and unconfessed sin continues through the generational line. Each generation casts a shadow on the next. Whenever the door of sin is opened to the devil, he is given a chance to tweak the DNA, mindsets, and bodies of the sinner that will be passed on to the next generation.

Cain was warned that if he did not do right, sin was crouching at his door. Sin does not miss a chance to enter your life to waylay you from your destiny. At the bodily death of each person, their children live under their shadow of unconfessed and unrepented sin. Medicine has long believed diseases are hereditary. Doctors ask about the health history of your blood family line. "Life" is in the blood, and the "death" is in the blood. Diabetes, cancer, heart disease, hearing and vision loss, and even skin diseases are shown to be hereditary. That is the devil's plan. But have no fear. You are not without redemption. Jesus Christ redeems us from the curses of the devil.

There are three areas of dysfunction to be addressed in the generational line,—body, mind, and emotions.

Present to the Lord any **physical diseases or malfunctions** in you and your family's past. Include in this list allergies, cancers, psoriasis, diabetes, bone diseases, disintegrating discs, etc. Confess that they exist, and repent for allowing them to live in your body or your children's body. Ask the Lord to show you where they originated. Repent of the sin that housed the disease. Fear, anxiety, stress, and guilt are common door openers to disease. People who lived in war-torn areas are exposed to toxic chemicals, constant fear, and anxiety that often develop emotionally connected diseases.

Lord, I admit these diseases exist in my family line: _____

I repent of the sin that housed these diseases: <u>anger, revenge, theft, drunkenness, gambling, etc.</u>_____.

I repent of past generations making agreements with <u>fear, anxiety, guilt, etc.</u>

Thank you for washing us clean.

Admit to holding **mindsets that are not in alignment with his Word** that cast a shadow on your life. Such things as "I have to work for everything I have," "God only answers some people's prayers," and "Once you've sinned, you are going to hell no matter what." These thoughts become your belief system that is often fostered by generations past. Think back on the stories you heard from grandparents and parents that only expressed fear and hopelessness. Ask the Holy Spirit to show you what mindsets overshadow you that keep you from God's best. Present to the Lord these emotions that control you—hate, sorrow, depression, anger, violence, apathy, etc. The Holy Spirit will show you what needs to be repented. Choose to repent. This is not a matter of feeling. It is a matter of shedding light on their presence in your life.

I repent of mindsets and emotions that have been contrary to your Word. List them:

_____

_____

Forgive your past generations for allowing these sins to beset you and future generations. By repentance and forgiveness, you can cut off the sinfulness of that generation. You cut off the *sinfulness*, not the people of that generation.

"Lord, on behalf of my generations past, I repent of allowing fear, anxiety, depression, and lies of the Enemy to live in our lives. Thank you that your Blood washes all generations. As I have repented and been forgiven of the sin, I declare that I no longer live under that generational shadow of sin. I declare that I now live under the shadow of the Almighty who will lead me in the path of righteousness."

The Enemy Lies!

And no wonder, for Satan himself masquerades as an angel of light.

(2 Corinthians 11:14)

Don't you hate it when somebody lies to you? You are told something that sounds good only to find out it was a lie.

Lying is a tactic the devil uses constantly.

He uses your voice, the voice of those you love, and the voice of strangers. The lies will come to you when you are most vulnerable. They come disguised as helpful advice, judgment, criticism, and put-downs. This does not mean everyone who speaks to you is a liar of the devil. This means you must be keenly aware of the truth and what God says about the situation.

Satan can also disguise himself as an angel of light. He will make everything look so good, and you jump to the conclusion that it is God. This is where it gets tricky. You must look at it all against the Word of God. Someone may pull you into a business scheme to make a lot of money, but it is a fraud. You must investigate to be sure all transactions are legal, and there is no illegal scheme involved. Search if there is an unfair advantage or profits that are unexplainable. Be wary. Do not accept the word of a "good friend." The devil can play the game of charades.

The devil will sabotage your self-talk. If you hear "Nobody loves you," you don't have to believe it. God loves you! The fact that you are awake, moving, and walking in the sun is evidence that God loves you.

"You are stupid and worthless" would be another lie the devil tells through the mouth of others. Since God does not make anything worthless, that is an outright lie. Unfortunately, if you do not challenge the thought with the Word of God, you can be swallowed up in the lie and anything connected to it.

The devil knows the principle of multiplication. Whatever you speak or think will multiply. Therefore, he will keep heaping on negative talk and hopelessness. These are common self-talk lies that become inner vows, as explained in the previous scenario. "I can never succeed," "I'm always going to do it wrong," "Everybody is against me," "God heals others, but He won't heal me," and "Why does something negative always happen to *me*?" These are lies that can set you on the road to destruction.

You have a choice to either believe the devil and repeat his lies or believe God and declare the wonders of God. If you keep thinking, "God is good to me," you will begin to see His goodness. You will develop a gratitude attitude, which will always usher in hope. Rejoice with others when they reap a blessing. Celebrating them will call in your blessing.

Fake News

The whole city was aroused, and the people came running from all directions. Seizing Paul, they dragged him from the temple, and immediately the gates were shut.[31] While they were trying to kill him, news reached the commander of the Roman troops that the whole city of Jerusalem was in an uproar. (Acts 21:30-31)

In this Bible account, Paul arrived in Jerusalem after preaching to the Gentiles in Asia. To counter the rumored belief that he had forsaken Jewish laws and customs, the elders encouraged him to go on a seven-day purification rite with four other men. Near the end of seven days, Paul entered the temple and the "fake news" about him started. They said, "This is the man who teaches all men everywhere against our people and our law and this place. And besides, he has brought Greeks into the temple area and defiled this holy place." None of that was true, but the crowd was stirred with contempt. They dragged Paul from the temple with the intent to kill him. The riot broke out based on what "somebody" said. It was fake news.

Fake news is meant to stir up emotions, not necessarily facts. It stirs confusion in belief systems and leads people to do dishonorable things—kill, destroy property, and defy authorities. Is this what we are seeing happen today? It's an old tactic by the devil to goad people into a frenzy. Nothing is new. Fake news is characterized by judgment, accusations, opinions, and truncated facts.

Fortunately for Paul, he was rescued by the Roman guard. He thought he could "reason" with the people by using history to set the stage for acceptance. However, once he declared he had a mandate from God to preach to Gentiles, the uproar erupted again—this time more violently. This new idea of God including everyone was outrageous. They, in essence, revolted against God.

God was changing their paradigm. They created fake news to support their position and give them an excuse to behave dishonorably. When God moves to change people's paradigm, they resist by creating fake news either by embellishing or subtracting facts. In today's world of the internet and fast communication, such tactics can create much damage to hide the truth God is speaking.

Fortunately, Paul was in the custody of the Roman guard after the riot in Jerusalem was fueled by fake news. Paul's Roman citizenship guaranteed him protection. In Caesarea, the Roman governmental headquarters, Governor Felix heard Paul's defense. For 2 years, this "fake news" issue was kept on hold with Paul in jail. Felix was finally replaced by Festus as governor, and the case was reopened. The fake news charges remained the same with a little more embellishment. The charges could not be proven. Paul made his defense trying to appeal to reason to no avail.

Paul, a Roman citizen, realized he was safer in the hands of the Roman guards, so he made his appeal to Caesar's court rather than risk his life to the crowds. The "fake news" rioters helped Paul get free passage to Rome, where he continued to preach the gospel. It was there in prison that he wrote his many letters to Christians.

All looked ugly, but God worked out His purpose for His glory.

Be careful of getting caught up in fake news. Facts can be twisted and sliced and diced to meet the desired narrative. The great danger of fake news is the action it ignites because it often stirs emotions into a frenzy. Look past the frenzy and see the substance of the issue. If it is not in alignment with the Word, then don't jump on the bandwagon. The Word of God is the sure foundation as written.

Prophecy, not Fortune Telling

For you can all prophesy in turn so that everyone may be instructed and encouraged. The spirits of prophets are subject to the control of prophets.

(1 Corinthians 14:31-32)

When prophecy is glamorized, it becomes dangerous because people start worshipping the prophet or the prophecy.

Prophecy should not be confused with fortune-telling. Fortune telling comes from the occult realm of the devil. Prophecy from God does not necessarily tell of the future. It is important to distinguish true prophecy from God or just someone's thoughts from his fleshly desires. True prophecy has three qualities.

(1) It encourages, brings correction (not judgment), edifies, or strengthens.

(2) It is in alignment with the Scriptures.

(3) It comes from the Holy Spirit.

A prophecy that detracts from God or leads people away from God is suspect. Let me clarify terms that are often used in the church that are confusing.

The **Office of the Prophet** is designated by the Body of Christ (Church). The officeholder is someone who has been trained and proven to be appointed by God. They have been tested to be truly serving God and edifying the Church. They are in a community with other trusted prophets. No one declares *himself* to be such a Prophet. They must be duly recognized by other prophets.

False prophets will offer a prophetic word for sale. The greater the money greater the prophecy will be. These prophets speak in the flesh and do not point you toward God. Often they operate out of the occult like witches. They point you away from God and His Word.

Prophets in training are true prophets who occasionally make mistakes while they are learning and maturing. They are in the "trial by fire" stage but are truly anointed by God. They focus on Jesus and usually are under the mentorship of a leader in the Church or other recognized Prophets.

The **religious spirit** adheres to legal rules and regulations, squelching creativity in the spirit. It orders every aspect of the spiritual life—no loud singing, no dancing, and no lifting hands. Kneel, bow, and stand at the correct times. This spirit plants fear in people who want freedom in Christ. You will not lose your salvation if you sneeze during prayer! Neither should you be shamed into dancing and shouting. You need to be in sync with the Holy Spirit.

The **Jezebel Spirit** operates in people who control by judgment and criticism to raise their position and influence. This spirit is a hard task-master that springs from idol worship. You can be operating in legalism and the Jezebel spirit without knowing it. Open your heart and eyes to the Holy Spirit to discern what spirits surround you. These steps will help you.

1. Pray in tongues. Worship with people who pray in the Holy Spirit. If you want to be a good tennis player, play with better tennis players, not golfers.
2. The gift of prophecy needs to be under spiritual supervision and allowed to mature. Be a rookie first.
3. Prophecy always aligns with the Word of God. If you are not sure, hold it until you have a confirmation.
4. Prophecy is to be released at the right time. Timing is important. You can control the timing of prophecy and how you deliver it. It does not move on automatic pilot. It respects human dignity.

5. When the spirit of prophecy is present, *all* can prophesy. Don't be afraid to join in encouraging and supporting.

Exercises:

1. Prophesy to yourself by speaking the Word to yourself by quoting the Scripture. "I am fearfully and wonderfully made." "The Lord watches my coming in and going out."
2. Prophesy to others by relating an appropriate scripture, a picture, a song, or a story. "God is holding you in the palm of his hand." "Like a sparrow, He will not let you fall."
3. Prophesy to a community is what you hear the Lord saying to them. "Go to the harvest field and work today." "The weapon formed against you will not prosper."

You too, can prophesy!

False Gods

You shall have no other gods before me. (Exodus 20:3)

When the Israelites were in Egypt, they were surrounded by a myriad of gods that were created by people to explain the different aspects of life or phenomena. The Egyptians did not have a concept of one god over all the earth, and neither did the Israelites, having been in bondage for 400 years. They were instructed to have only one god, but they did not understand the fullness of Him. Yahweh had to teach them that He was The One and only God of all creation looking out for them.

To move their focus onto Him, He demanded that there be no other God. They were not accustomed to an invisible god. The gods they knew, whether they worshiped them or not, were always some visible ornament or figure as the center of focus. They created the idol according to how they saw the idol's function. Some were of animals, some fanciful creatures, and some were things in nature such as the moon, a tree, or a rock. God did not want them to focus on these objects because he was teaching them to know his powerful *presence* and not his image. His presence came in a cloud by day and fire by night—their protector, leader, and provider.

Today, many other religions still erect idols to have a visual and tactile representation of the god they want to worship. These idols are limited by men's hands and imaginations. Unfortunately, they are given power through worship. Some idols represent goodness, and some are an object of fear and wickedness. People build customs of offerings, rituals, and lifestyles to reflect the god.

Because Jesus is the Creator of the universe, He cannot be contained in an image. We may have representations, such as the cross or a crucifix, of Him to focus our minds on what He did for us, but we do not ascribe power to the representation. Any other human that has died and is exalted to the level of a god is an idol. There is a difference between recognizing saints for their sacrificial lives and "praying to them" and expecting them to do something for you. Ascribing power to them is idolatry. Idolatry is dangerous because it opens up a spiritual portal for Satan to use the disguise and usurp your worship that belongs to God alone. You were created to worship God, not idols.

Hard idols, though seemingly worthless, are connected with the occult world. They invite witchcraft, voodoo, satanic rituals, spells, and other occult powers into your life. Trinkets such as a rabbit's foot, 4-leaf clovers, and a lock of mom's hair become idols when we trust in them for "good luck."

Soft idols are things of the world that you might raise above God, such as your job, spouse, children, money, and fame. This idolatry grows as you worship them and sacrifice to them. These idols separate you from God. You can pour all your money and time into these idols that cannot bless you as God can. The values become compromised.

Besides physical idols, people create virtual idols. Anything that consumes all your attention, wealth, and energy can be an idol. If you use education, family, sports, drugs, alcohol, food, and money to fill your spiritual, physical, mental, or emotional needs, you have created an idol. Only God can fill your emptiness. Even a lie can be an idol when you serve it. "I can never be successful" is a mindset that can be served by constant self-sabotage. "I always make mistakes" will always cause just missing the mark of any endeavor. An idol will never be satisfied, and you will keep serving that idol to keep it happy unless you bring it down from its pedestal. Seeking fulfillment through other sources is idolatry.

The most dangerous idol is self.

When you exalt yourself to the level that you believe even God cannot fix your mistakes or redeem you, you have made yourself an idol. If you believe that you have to work for or earn your salvation, you have made yourself an idol. Your efforts then become more powerful than God's love. If you cannot forgive yourself for anything, then you believe you are more powerful than God.

If you wonder if you might have been serving idols, ask yourself, "Do these things give me life or steal life from me?" Idols take. God gives. Idols take your energy, your self-worth, your money, and your peace of mind. God gives you confidence, power, wealth, and peace.

How to bring down an idol? Repent and Forgive.

Lord, I repent of worshiping the idol of _____. I repent of serving its lies and raising it above you. I forgive myself for agreeing with the idol. I now choose to bring that idol down and submit it to your cross. Set me free. I choose to worship only you.

Wolf Disguises

Be alert and of sober mind. Your enemy the devil prowls around like a roaring lion looking for someone to devour. (1Peter 5:8)

Wolves in Sheep's clothing refers to spiritual issues and everyday life issues. There are scams and fraud schemes that would draw you into the devil's traps if you are unaware. Remember, sheep's clothing always looks benign, profitable, or good. Watch out for some of the common ones.

Credit Card fraud begins with something "free." Most people take notice of a deal or something for free. Rarely will you find someone who says they want to pay more. That would happen only if there were only one. You can find offers for everything from steaks and free groceries to cosmetics and health remedies. These offers will ask you to pay for shipping to get your prize. Very often, the item is of very poor quality, is fake, or you never receive it. Meanwhile, the merchant has your name, address, email, phone, and credit card info. These are all open doors to *credit card fraud*.

Identity Theft is more than someone using your credit card. If it were, the easy fix would be to cancel your credit card. Identity theft will ruin your credit rating, your mortgage standing, your job prospect, and even travel eligibility. Some thieves will use your photo and your career to scam others to bolster their credibility. Rectifying this is costly and very time-consuming, not to include the angst and anxiety. This is why there is identity theft insurance. However, the prevention starts with YOU.

Social Media is great for keeping in contact with friends, but it can be a trap for unsuspecting and indiscriminating users. Fundraising requests will pull at your heartstrings and your wallet. Scammers can build fake stories of hard times and unfortunate health situations to then request money. Not only do they get into your wallet, but they use your identity for character smearing, alter your photos, and make you look like the enemy.

Social Media can also be an open door to human trafficking. If a stranger wants to "meet you in person," be very careful. This could be a real wolf in sheep's clothing. Too many youngsters and "friendship starved" people are kidnapped, abused, or lured into bondage relationships. This could be the start of sex, drug, or child trafficking.

Most *tech support* agencies ask for verification of your identity if you are already registered with them. When you call a third-party tech support company, they will ask for your personal information to build a file for you. You must be sure to vet these companies, so you are not lured into a scam whereby you are giving too much information. Too much information will include your Social Security number, your birth date, your driver's license number, and your city of birth. Do not give your bank account number if you have to pay a fee. With a credit card, you can reverse the charges through the credit card company if necessary. Be aware of monthly payment offers. They usually mean you will be automatically charged even if you do not use their services. These payments are often difficult to stop.

The Association of Mature American Citizens Foundation points out common scams used against elders.

It is good to know that the *Internal Revenue Service* (IRS) does not use phone contact or email for serious issues. Fear gets seniors to give out their social security numbers and other important information. You are told that you are being audited, you owe back taxes, or you are being investigated for fraud. The law-abiding citizen would be threatened. Elders who do not have anyone to assist them easily comply.

Another important piece of information to know is that the *Social Security Administration* also communicates officially by mail and paper trail. There are fake emails and phone scams to threaten the seniors' Social Security status. Although the SSA communicates by mail, it's also important to inspect the letter that "looks" like Social Security mail. Somewhere on the envelope or the letter, there might be a small print disclaimer. Do not call the phone number in the letter. Look up the phone number yourself or log in directly from the web to check out the issue.

I once received a letter indicating I needed to record the Deed of Trust to my home. This company, with an official government-sounding name and official-looking letterhead, offered to record for a fee. Fortunately, I knew such a transaction was free for citizens. After inspecting the letter, I found it on the envelope in very small print on the return address, "not a government document." Most people open a letter and discard the envelope without inspecting it. Tricky!

Unfortunately, unscrupulous repair contractors prey on unsuspecting Seniors who need repair and construction help to upkeep their homes. Helpless seniors are only too happy to have help. These people usually have a smooth sales talk, offer such a deal, then "discover" more things to be done. The things I have found useful are to ask for the license, the insurance coverage, and the official business name. If they cannot provide in writing a valid license number and insurance coverage, it is a risk. The official business name allows you to check the Better Business Bureau. This is not to say there are no legitimate businesses. You just need to be aware of any wolf in sheep's clothing.

I had a salesperson sell me cable and Wi-Fi services from a reputable company in the area, so I did not question the offer. Unfortunately, when the company came to install it, they could not because the salesperson sold a service that was not available in my area. After weeks of follow-up with numerous phone calls, I managed to get a refund and end the mess.

The Grandparents' special targets the love of their life, their grandchildren. The worse scam that pulls on the heartstrings of the elderly is the "grandchild is in trouble" scenario. A news story told of grandparents who received a call saying that their grandchild who lived far away was in trouble and needed $10,000 to be extricated. The story was fabricated by thieves with the caveat that calling the police would jeopardize the child's safety. The money was to be "dropped off in cash" at a certain time and place to free the child. It sounded like a movie. The grandparents believed it and dropped off the money, only to find out later it was a scam. Their beloved grandchild was always safe.

Remember, the devil plans to kill, steal, and destroy anything and everything. It is your job to guard and protect the things God has given you, whether things, services, or people. When you do that, The Lord will put his additional protection around you, but you must be careful and alert. The wolf disguise comes in many forms. Be alert!!

CHAPTER 5

Living as Heirs of the Most High

In the Lord's Prayer, we say, "thy Kingdom come on earth as it is in heaven." God reigns in Heaven. To reign is to hold royal office and govern according to the king's laws. He intends for us is to reign like him over the earth to enforce the laws of the King of Kings, Jesus Christ. Reigning is a sacred privilege and an awesome responsibility for those who are under our care. Earthly kings must learn how to reign, so we too must train to reign on earth with our Heavenly King.

Your new salvation life requires growth and some pruning to grow into maturity. A farmer plants the seeds and nurtures the young seedlings until they reach maturity to produce fruit. In the process, there are transitions, seasons, and fruit-producing times. Maturity brings you to the point of producing abundance in your life. Jesus Christ came into the world to give life so that we might have it abundantly. (John 10:10)

You are "the head and not the tail, above and not beneath." (Deuteronomy 28:13) You have outward, inward, and attitudinal characteristics linked to reigning. The following scenarios prepare you to reign on the earth with the King of Kings.

Look at Life from a Soccer game

*Be very careful, then, how you live—
not as unwise but as wise.* (Ephesians 5:15)

As I watched 11-year-olds play soccer, I heard the coach say, "We need to learn how to play soccer, not just run around!"

I noticed that my grandson, with his inexhaustible energy, was one of the most eager players on the team. I listened as best I could when the referees called the plays, and the little I had learned about soccer rules returned to my mind. The referees called the plays. The game stopped each time there was an infraction of the rules. When the ball went out of bounds, the game stopped. The last to touch the ball determined who would have the next possession. The team with the throw-in from the boundary line to resume play had the advantage. The team with better playing skills—dribbling, kicking, and blocking—would advance more quickly, and the opportunities for shooting goals increased.

I thought, "This is like life. Learn to play the game and don't just run around."

- God calls the plays.
- The game stops when there is an infraction of the rules (sin).
- When you go out of bounds (too far away from God), the game stops.
- The ones with the next "throw in" (gets up and continues) have the advantage.
- The ones with the better playing (life) skills would advance more quickly.
- The opportunities for shooting goals (success) increase.

PRAYER: "Lord, instruct me in wisdom and lead me along straight paths." Equip me to play "Life" on the field that you gave me. Amen."

Living as Heirs of the Most High   119

Transitions

Yet he (Abraham) did not waver through unbelief regarding the promise of God, but was strengthened in his faith and gave glory to God, being fully persuaded that God had the power to do what he had promised.

(Romans 4:20-21)

Transitions are always uncomfortable because you are moving from the familiar to the unfamiliar. You are excited and nervous at the same time. Going from elementary school to Junior High or from High School to College/Job are transitions in early life. From being single to married, childless to parenthood, or staff to supervisor are adult transitions. This is a time of transition for everyone in God's Kingdom plan for the earth. You are not expected to go it alone when you decide to step up to a new level of discipleship. You are transitioning from an old way of life to a Kingdom of God way of life. You can prepare to navigate transitions smoothly. Here are some transition tips from the Bible.

1. **When you don't know what to do, worship.** (1 Samuel 30)

David was just ejected from fighting alongside the Philistines. He and his men returned to Ziklag to find their homes raided and the women and children kidnapped. Instead of wringing his hands and crying, "Why did this happen to me?" he worshipped God. He turned to God for directions. God gave a plan to pursue and recover all. He did.

2. **Let God cleanse your lips and heart before you represent Him.**

(Isaiah 6:1) Isaiah was preparing to represent God before the people. He knew his lips and heart had to be clean before taking on the task. God gave him a new level of speaking on His behalf by cleansing his lips.

3. **Repent** (Matthew 3:2)

Every new adventure with God begins with repentance leaving behind old ways, old thinking, and old expectations. God is starting something new in you. God's plan for you is for good and not for evil. He is always good. Get ready for something new to bloom in your life.

4. **Seek private prayer time with God.** (Luke 5:16)

Shift to a personal source of revelation and prayer. Jesus went to a private place to pray, by himself, not in the synagogue. He did not depend on scheduled services to commune with God. This transition is for you to receive guidance for yourself.

5. **Allow others to minister to you.** (John 11:43-44)

You are not expected to be on this journey alone. God will provide companions and mentors, healers, and deliverers. After being raised from the dead, Lazarus needed the grave clothes removed. Those who witnessed the miracle were instructed to unwrap him, not be just observers. When you allow others to minister to you, your grave clothes can be removed.

6. **Join small group prayer.** (Matthew 18:20)

When you join with at least one other person in prayer, you multiply the power of your prayers and your kinship with those in agreement. There is power in the prayer of agreement. Although more will be better, it only takes two or three to agree.

7. **Focus on being unified in the Church.** (Acts 9:31)

The Church is the institution that is entrusted with the work of Jesus. As recipients of His Salvation gifts and as his followers, join with other followers in unity. Whatever God calls you to do, connect with His empowered group. When the disciples were in unity, the Church had peace and victory.

8. **Rise with the boldness of the Holy Spirit to carry out your assignment.**

(Romans 15:13) You have a purpose and plan from God found in His Perfect Will. That Perfect Will includes all of those who work to bring his Kingdom on earth. It will take courage and boldness to advance.

When you see transitions as an adventure, you will be able to enjoy yourself regardless of the difficulty. God will never leave you or forsake you. He provides all you need to succeed. Keep moving.

After I was caring for two young boys, 19 months apart, I had to transition from being a career music teacher to a full-time mom. When out in the career world, I could talk to other adults with the same interests and had stimulating conversations with other teachers. When I began to stay home with my children, the stimulating conversations turned from me to me. It seemed like I was always diapering, wiping noses or rear ends, preparing food, and waiting for their nap time. If they napped together, I was in luck. Then I could do laundry, even talk on the phone with a friend, or read the Bible. Talking with friends who had traveled through this child-rearing stage of life was a great encouragement. They would listen to me, pray with me, and let me see the humor in some of the situations. There was never a time when I said, "I have arrived," but I grew into the role and the new life. It's amazing how you can have private time with the Lord while in the shower. There came a time when the unfamiliar became the familiar, and I got comfortable being who I was meant to be in that season of my life.

Begin On the Outside

*Put your outdoor work in order
and get your fields ready;
after that, build your house.*

(Proverbs 24:27)

Horse races begin at the gates with horses and jockeys at the ready position. Any horse that is not in the gate with a riding jockey is not in a position to start. At the sound of the gun, the gates fly open, and the horses take off. The same scenario is set for track runners, ice skating racers, ski racers, and even marathon runners. They all start the race the same way—*in position.*

When you accept Jesus Christ into your life as Lord and Savior, you agree to go to the starting gate of life with Christ. Unfortunately, some agree to run the race with Christ but never go to the starting gate. They choose to continue their lives in old pastures.

Life with Christ consists of many short races. Some test our skills, some test our endurance, and others test our obedience. They all culminate in the life-long pursuit of destiny. The ones who choose to train can endure. Just as your body needs to be *in condition* for long races, your spirit and soul need to be conditioned for the race so that you can endure, persevere, and skillfully navigate life's challenges. How should you start building holiness to be in condition for the challenges of life?

Begin to hang out with *mature* Christians and imitate them. Paul tells the Corinthians (1 Corinthians 4:16-17) to imitate him and Timothy as examples. See how they talk, how they work, how they treat others, how they pray, how they study the Word, and how they worship. We learn dance steps by following others until we can do it on our own. Why not follow in the Christian life? Jesus said, "Follow me."

None of these tips cost money, but they will cost your willfulness or laziness. You need to start somewhere, and since life with Christ involves a community, you need first to remove barriers to relationships. Do not be deceived into thinking that others will look beyond your exterior presentation to find the "nice you" inside. Most people do not have the patience. Work on the outside first because that is where first impressions are made.

1. Choose wholesomeness in what people see and hear from you.
2. Speak plainly without sarcastic remarks, foul expletives, and repulsive phrases.
3. Use positive body language without smirking, sneering, mocking, frowning, and eye-rolling.
4. Smile. Laugh joyfully. Stand and sit with respect.
5. Dress respectfully to yourself and others. Be clean. Wear clean clothes. Avoid sexually provocative attire.
6. Keep your surroundings clean, such as your car, office, and home.
7. Be responsible for your finances. Pay your bills on time. Don't cause others to avoid you because you always need to borrow money.
8. Take charge of your education, whether it is formal learning, job training, learning a language, or a personal skill such as crafts, athletics, and health. Today's information highway is literally at your fingertips.

In my work as a pastoral counselor, I need to discern who I can help and who I cannot help. Some have believed they can be "casual" with God and speak with filthy language and negative attitudes. It is very difficult to help them because they are just looking for affirmation of their bad behaviors. Their exterior barriers push away any empathy or any heart listening I might try to extend.

Remember, you are representing Christ to reign with Him. When you start behaving with royal dignity, the doors will open for you.

You Can Choose

This day I call the heavens and the earth as witnesses against you that I have set before you life and death, blessings and curses. Now choose life, so that you and your children may live. (Deuteronomy 30:19)

There are some things God determines for you according to your destiny. No one chose their parents, place of birth, date of birth, gender, or color. But, did you know you can choose the kind of person you want to be?

The first and greatest gift God gave to you is the gift of free will.

Although His desire is for you to reign with him, you are not forced to reign with him. You can choose your way or what someone else decides. You can either choose to obey God or not to obey Him. In all cases, you have the final say.

The Natural Person is born of the flesh with no connection to salvation at birth. This person absorbs ideas and ways that the world tells him are best. "Everybody else does it" is his favorite song. This person is always looking out for his own gain regardless of the consequences on others.

A willful and rebellious person chooses to live just as he wants and makes choices according to the flesh and the world or his idea of what's good. This could be a combination of good and bad. The rich young ruler went away sad because he didn't want to do the things Jesus advised. Ever tried to help someone who didn't want your help? Their willfulness blocks you just as it will block out God.

The Saved Person has chosen to accept Jesus as Savior, the Messiah. This person now has the opportunity to be cleansed from sin through the Blood of Jesus in repentance and forgiveness. He *has the means* of warding off the wages of sin, which is death. This death can be in relationships, finances, physical or mental health. The question becomes, "Does he use his opportunity to become a child of the *Living* God?"

A Sanctified Person chooses to allow the Holy Spirit to show him what he needs to repent and what and who he needs to forgive. He chooses to be holy and righteous. Zacchaeus chose righteousness when he pledged to make restitution for cheating others. This person takes steps to line up with the ways of God. (Luke 19:1-10)

An Anointed Person chooses to be a disciple. A disciple is dedicated beyond being sanctified. He does due diligence in developing and growing his skills and talents. He accepts correction, wisdom from others, and mentoring. As he walks in ways of righteousness, the Holy Spirit will add to him supernatural power and grace so that he will excel and show the glory of God in all things. God anoints to show off quality. The anointing is not an accident. Paul was a highly educated and skilled debater, but his speaking was more than intellectual. Paul's preaching in the Areopagus made a great impact because of the anointing.

An Empowered Person chooses obedience: When you surrender to God whatever abilities you have, God will sovereignly move with power. Philip was supernaturally translated to the Ethiopian's carriage and was again transported to Samaria. (Acts 8: 26-39) That is supernatural empowerment. God chooses the time and place. You can make yourself available and be obedient. When you are empowered, you can heal, prophesy, impart, declare, move mountains, intercede, pray, and even exhort. When you speak, everybody listens. Miracles happen.

The Lord told a pastor's wife to do cartwheels on the platform at one point in the service. She thought that was crazy, but she was obedient. She didn't know there was a cynical man in the audience who challenged the Lord with something he thought was absurd. "I won't believe this is real unless I see someone do cartwheels on the stage," he said. Because of the woman's obedience, that man was convinced God was real. That was an empowering moment.

When you choose to obey God, you will reign with him and have the great privilege of touching others on His behalf. His Kingdom will come from heaven to earth.

Fasting

*But **Daniel** resolved not to defile himself with the royal food and wine, and he asked the chief official for permission not to defile himself this way.* (Daniel 1:8)

Fasting is a discipline over the body to produce a spiritual gain. When you fast, you bring your body or fleshly desires under the control of your spirit. Fasting usually refers to food. Many religions besides Christians practice fasting. Muslims practice fasting during Ramadan. Christians usually consider Lent as a time of fasting. Hunger is a powerful urge that can propel you to gorge or push food away. When you fast, you need to be mindful of physical effects such as dehydration and personal health conditions.

The "Daniel fast" is mostly thought of as a fast of eating just fruits and vegetables. The purpose of the fast is to take control of your body through your eating. We are told that Daniel and his companions requested this diet in the Babylonian court. After ten days, they proved to be healthier, smarter, and wiser than the others who ate food from the king's table.

On a closer look at the first chapter of Daniel, we see that the king worshipped the idols of the Babylonians. The food at the king's table was usually food sacrificed to idols. The food, usually meats and wine, were libations to the idols of Babylon. To keep themselves clean of any idol worship, Daniel and his companions requested just fruits and vegetables. Those would be the safest foods. The Jews had strict dietary rules on the preparation of meats which probably the king's court did not observe. Meats are made kosher by the blood being drained from the animal. The meat from the king's table could have been of animals considered by the Jews as "unclean" or animals already dead when found. This not only had a health effect but also a spiritual meaning if the food was first offered to idols, as was the custom.

Daniel and his companions were found to be smarter and wiser than all the magicians and enchanters. Yes, of course, since other men were relying on demons as their source. Daniel and his companions were already men of high intellect, comely looks, and noble birth. They were preserving their gifts from God and behaving in a godly manner. Faithfulness to Jehovah was their watchword. This was a test of discipline. Because of their faithfulness, God gave them additional knowledge and understanding of many things, including Daniel's ability to interpret dreams.

There are other things to fast besides food or meat only.

1. Fast from things that glorify idols like materialism, money, fame, education, drugs, sex, and ego.
2. Fast from exalting the devil in horror movies, torture, crime, and evil deeds.
3. Fast from idle talk, gossip, foul language, judgments, name-calling, and slander.
4. Fast from anything that brings God down. Self-righteousness, self-promotion, arrogance, and anything filthy that does not glorify God.

Fasting meals but still engaging in pornography, horror movies, gossip, foul language, slander, and self-promotion is futile. God does not honor sin no matter how much you fast your food. Do not be deceived! You cannot expect to emerge as smarter and wiser, blessed by God just because you didn't eat.

While you are fasting foods, you are consuming things through your eyes, ears, mind, and mouth. Consume good literature, music, film, and godly talk. If you do, you will have knowledge and understanding of all kinds of literature and learning. When examined by the world, you will be ten times better than magicians or enchanters. Fasting should be spiritually profitable and not just fashionable. There is more than the food involved in fasting. Feast on the fruit of the spirit as found in Galatians 5:22—love, joy, peace, patience, kindness, goodness, faithfulness, gentleness, and self-control.

How long and what to fast is best dictated by the Lord. A community fast is one in which a group agrees to fast for a certain time for a specific goal. Individual fasts can be prolonged over days or intermittent such as every Wednesday. Because fasting is a means of bringing forth a closer relationship with the Lord, it should be directed by the Lord.

Teach us to pray

One day Jesus was praying in a certain place. When he finished, one of his disciples said to him, "Lord, teach us to pray, just as John taught his disciples." (Luke 11:1)

Prayer is earnest communication with a deity. It is the major activity of people who represent the royal family of God. Through prayer, you communicate with the King of Kings to bring heaven to earth for yourself and others. Bringing heaven on earth is the Christian's assignment.

The disciples noticed Jesus prayed regularly and had an amazing relationship with the Father. Jesus prayed purposefully "in a certain place." His certain place was not "on the way to" or when it was "convenient." "A certain place" can be a special chair, at home, at church, in the park, or even in your car.

When I was employed, the spacious back seat of my Volkswagen van became my "certain place." I parked my car in the shade of the parking garage, where there would be little traffic at lunchtime. I spent my lunch hour eating and then praying purposefully. Some days I would walk on the roof of the parking structure, singing and praying aloud. I think the only person who saw me was the security guard watching the garage monitor.

Notice the scripture says "when He finished." There is a start and stop to a prayer session. Yes, we are told to pray continually, but there is a kind of prayer that has a specific purpose. Grace before a meal or the invocation opening a meeting are specific prayers. Yet, there are times when you push forward for a specific event or situation. These also have start and stop times or else you will be overwhelmed and scattered in whatever normal duties you may have. Ruminating over a situation is not prayer. It is worry.

Jesus tells us what to *say*, not think. The mouth is linked to the heart. What you say will be what you believe. Conversely, what you believe is what you will say. What you want to affect, you must verbalize.

Jesus gave the example of the Lord's Prayer which many have said hundreds of times. It warrants deep thought and respect. "Our Father, who is in heaven, hallowed be thy name. Thy Kingdom come. Thy will be done on earth as it is in heaven. Give us today our daily bread. Forgive us our sins as we forgive those who sin against us. Lead us not into temptation but deliver us from evil."

The power of this prayer does not deserve rote recitation.

- First, who are you addressing? *The Father.*
- What is His characteristic? *He is holy.*
- Where does He dwell? *In heaven.*
- What does He do there? *He reigns in his kingdom.*
- We are addressing the realm where God and the heavenly hosts dwell in perfect worship and harmony. *We are asking that this holy kingdom of heaven come to earth.*
- Earth is the realm where our *daily bread is needed.*
- *Sin and death block* the transmission from heaven to earth.
- Temptation is the *lure to sin.*
- *Forgiveness is the secret strategy* that removes the power of sin and death.

You are to ask boldly of the Father regardless of circumstances. Many fail to ask for something because they decide that "He is too busy," "He would not want to help anyway," or "We don't deserve it."

Ask, seek, and knock. To **ask**, you have to verbalize. Verbalization gives clarity and power to our request. **Seek** is to purposefully engage in activities that will bring about the request. **Knock** means to expect a door to be opened so you can take hold of the prize.

Prayer is *not* wishful thinking. Wishful thinking is to yourself or nobody in particular. Prayer is directed to your heavenly Father, who wants to hear from you. Yes, the scripture says he knows what we need before we ask, but it also tells us we need to ask and not wish for it.

How to Pray for Yourself

You have not because you ask not. (James 4:2)

If you pray with these phrases "if it be your will," "would you…," "could you…," you are speaking from wishful thinking. Praying from faith is standing on the promises of God as found in the Bible. He is a faithful God and will perform what he says he will do.

Petitionary prayer is lifting prayers for yourself. The Enemy might tell you, "It is selfish to pray for yourself." However, since you are the one who is with you 24/7, you would best know what you need and want. If you are declaring the promises of God and the fulfillment of your destiny, you are doing the right thing. The Bible says, ask and you shall receive. (*Matthew 7:7*) Whatever you ask in my name I shall do it". (*John 14:14*)

Here are some examples of proper petitions.

1. "Lord, you have put into my heart the desire to become a doctor. Because you are my Provider, I am trusting you to provide all that I need to reach that goal. You will give me the money, the college acceptances, and the contacts. I lean on you for the discipline to study and learn and the perseverance to complete the course you set before me."

2. Lord, you have put in my heart to care for orphans. Show me where, how, and when I should move forward. Bring me the people you will use to provide the funds, the facilities, and those who will partner with me in this endeavor—teachers, doctors, social workers, nannies, maintenance workers, lawyers, and loving parents. I am depending on you to give me the perseverance and wisdom to complete this destiny."

3. Lord, I desire to fulfill my destiny as a mother to my three children. Remind me that I must constantly look to you in all

my life's challenges so that my children will learn by example. Show me how to instill the Word in their lives. Let me be there for them. As you are my heavenly Father, let them see you in me. When I make mistakes, thank you Lord that I can come to you in repentance to be forgiven and given a new chance to make a godly difference in their lives.

So you see, a petition isn't just asking God for a new car, a vacation to Hawaii, or a promotion in your job. Your heavenly Father will find pleasure in giving you those things as they fit in your capacity to use them to his glory.

Before asking Him for more money, ask yourself if you have demonstrated your ability to handle what you already have. Do you save for emergencies? Do you tithe? Do you pay your bills on time, or are you in debt? Do you spend more than you earn? Do you prioritize your spending? These are all questions you must answer and take action on for God to fulfill your request for more money.

Another common request is for a better job. How well do you do the one you have? Are you reliable? Can you be trusted? Do you only do what is required or are you resourceful and helpful in blessing the company with your ideas? Do you complain about everything:—hours, conditions, breaks, vacations? Are you a blessing to the company? Do you get along with your boss and co-workers? You don't earn a better job. You qualify for it. He wants the glory.

One day I had to take my son to an important appointment after school at a place that usually is a two-hour drive away. This was the only day we could do this. I picked him up as soon as school was out and headed to downtown Los Angeles. I did not pray, "Oh, Lord, I hope I get there on time." I prayed, "Lord, you opened the Red Sea for Moses; you can open this freeway for me. You know when I must arrive at the office. I am trusting you." I drove calmly without speeding or weaving through rush hour traffic and got there a half-hour early.

When I told others of this happening, they said it was a miracle! I was translated like Philip was in the Bible. I believe it was a miracle, just like the parting of the Red Sea!

    The Lord always delights when you give him the glory. He does not count how many times you say Hallelujah. He desires that you shine with his character in all things. Sometimes he puts you in difficult situations so you can be his ambassador in dark places. Your light should shine brighter with every trial, not dimmer. *"Let your light shine before men so that they may see your good works and glorify your Father in heaven."* (Matthew 5:16)

Doubt and Unbelief

Even after Jesus had performed so many signs in their presence, they still would not believe in him.

(John 12:37)

"Help overcome my unbelief" were the words of the father whose son was delivered from epilepsy. He had come to the disciples for help, and none of them could get results. When Jesus arrived on the scene, Jesus cast out the demon, and the boy was set free. The dad watched the whole thing and found it hard to believe this miracle had happened.

Unbelief sets in when you see the wonders of God and yet do not believe He can do that. The Israelites saw God part the Red Sea, rain manna from heaven, and bring water out of the rock. Still, they would not believe God could take them into the Promised Land to conquer the giants. Because of their unbelief, they wandered in the desert for 40 years until the next generation, who did not see all the miracles, believed by faith God would do as He said He would.

Doubt, on the other hand, does not have any evidence. Thomas doubted Jesus rose from the dead because He was not there to see the resurrected Jesus as the other eleven disciples and the women did. He wanted evidence. When Jesus appeared to Him personally in the second meeting with the disciples, Thomas believed and did not need any more evidence.

When I am in the gym, I doubt I can run a mile in 10 minutes. There is no evidence I have the strength and stamina. The practice runs do not point to such a success. However, there is evidence that I can dead lift a 100-pound barbell. Those who watch me are in unbelief when they still say they don't believe it. Those who doubt I can will stand in disbelief when they see it.

Look for evidence. When you see the goodness of God, believe He will continue to be good. When you see miracles, you will be able to cast off unbelief. Don't let unbelief erode your faith in God, keeping you from going forward with Him.

Mercy and Grace

Turn to me and have mercy on me, as you always do to those who love your name. (Psalm 119:132)

Mercy is God's gift when we are either the victim of harm or a receiver of punishment. It's God's mercy that saved students from the fire. It is God's mercy that saves you from being killed in an auto accident. When our hearts are right with God, His mercy brings a lesser consequence. An accountant pled guilty to embezzlement. He repented before the Lord and was ready to accept his punishment. His lawyer told him to "bring his toothbrush" on the day of trial because all the evidence pointed toward an immediate jail sentence. At the trial, the punishment given was 2 years parole, and employment restricted to jobs that did not involve handling money. Both he and his lawyer were surprised and thankful for mercy.

Grace is a Free Gift, Not a Free Ride

*My grace is sufficient for you,
for my power is made perfect in weakness.*

(2 Corinthians 12:9)

Grace is the empowering spirit that allows you to accomplish more than you could on your own strength. When you find yourself weak, inadequate for the job, or not sure you can finish the task, get ready to receive grace. Usually, grace does not come in truckloads before you move forward. It comes *as* you move forward. Grace comes when you are faced with challenging situations. It's by the grace of God that medical students make it through an internship. It's by the grace of God that jet pilots keep their cool to bring in a disabled plane. It was by the grace of God that Captain Sully landed on the Hudson. It was by the grace of God that first-responders rescued people from the Twin Towers.

The champion golfer, Tiger Woods, was involved in a horrific auto accident that could have killed him. He was so badly injured and there was doubt he would play again. It was God's **mercy** that kept him alive. It was God's **grace** that brought him through rehabilitation to be able to play again like a champion.

Many people were injured in the 2013 Boston Marathon when a bomb went off. By God's mercy, no more people were killed or injured and many were rescued. By God's grace, the injured were healed. By God's grace, those with life-changing injuries have persevered.

Early in our marriage, my husband wanted to have somewhat formal dinner parties. His dad was a Lt. Colonel in the army, and entertaining was customary for them. My husband thought every family had sit-down dinners for guests. I grew up in a family that had family and friends over frequently, but no formal entertaining. With my husband's hospitality skills and my cooking, by God's grace, we became a hospitality team. Through the years, we have hosted many formal and informal dinners, weddings for friends, and fundraising events in our home. We have hosted international exchange students and foreign travelers. The Lord provided us with a large home and finances to carry out his plan to show his glory. It is by His grace that we continue to do these things to bless many people.

Are you wisely using the grace given to you? You will have the grace to pay attention to your children's needs, care for an elderly parent, and strengthen your marriage. God's grace will be with you.

Remember His Mercy endures forever and His Grace is all-sufficient.

Sharing God's Glory

*Now if we are children, then we are heirs—
heirs of God and co-heirs with Christ,
if indeed we share in his sufferings in order
that we may also share in his glory.*

(Romans 8:17)

Victory is the final and complete supremacy in a battle, either over an opponent or obstacles. There are victories in elections, boxing matches, or even illness. One thing we know for sure is that there is contending before the victory. Victory is not automatic, nor are we to be passive and wait for it to "happen." God promises us victory, but that victory is assured only when we are in the will and timing of God in the earth realm.

Three things you must remember about God's victory:

(1) **God decides who, where, when, what and how.** He is sovereign. Do not try to dictate when the victory should happen. Do not be discouraged, impatient, and even angry because it did not happen the way you envisioned it.

(2) **God speaks, you obey, and the victory is assured.** Double guessing God is a sure way of delaying or waylaying your victory.

(3) **You only enter into victory by the obedience of faith.** Jesus entered victory when he obediently went to the cross. Not all obedience takes you to the cross. Be careful that you don't sometimes offer God "alternatives" for achieving your victory. Obey his directions.

Steps to victory:

(1) **Salvation** gives you deliverance from sin and death. Through repentance and forgiveness, sin no longer can entangle your life.

(2) **Righteousness** brings personal integrity that guarantees victory. Righteousness can overcome because the wages of sin are removed. Repentance and forgiveness make you blameless, therefore in righteousness with God.

(3) **Peace** comes when you are in right standing with God. You enjoy total well-being—health, financial, mental, emotional, intellectual, etc. The circumstances may be in upheaval, but you can still enjoy total well-being.

You are more than a conqueror through Him. You are an Heir. Conquerors take over territory that is and never was theirs.

Heirs reclaim what was rightfully theirs in the first place.

They are influencers and reformers who restore the territory to the greatness that God originally intended. Take back your health, and restore it. Take back your family, and restore it. Take back your financial wealth, and restore it. Take back your mind, and restore it to the mind of Christ. As a warrior in Christ, take back the earth that is the Lord's and restore it to the glory of the Father.

When recovering from a neck injury after an auto accident, I had to keep my mind focused on Jesus to take back my health. I followed the doctor's directions and let the Lord heal me His way. It was not my idea to lay flat on my back for 100 days, but I did as I was instructed. I was healed with no lingering side effects. I had peace during the process and recovered total mobility.

CHAPTER 6

Divine Partnership

God says He knew you before the world began. That's a very long time ago. He also says that he *formed* you in your mother's womb. You were no accident. He formed you carefully and meticulously. He also decided when and where in history you would be on earth to accomplish a purpose in the world that would bring Him glory. He decided on your color, gender, physical makeup, and even your birthdate. How awesome is that?

People talk about the "end of time" when there is no end of time. God does not operate in time. Time only measures *your* existence. Too often, you think God is bound by time like you are. You worry about when He will show up or whether He knows how you are not having a good time. As you try to grasp the vastness of God, you realize how finite you are and how great God is. God is in the past, present, and future all at once. He knows how things will conclude before they even begin. He is Omnipresent.

What God Will NOT Do

Jesus replied, "What is impossible with man is possible with God." (Luke 18:27)

I know it sounds like a contradiction to say nothing is impossible for God and He can do anything. Yet there are things that God *will not* do. Although He can, He will only act on what is within his will. He will always be true to his Word and will not back down on his promises to you. When God says "always," He means always. When He says "never," He means never. Since He is the God of eternity, both of those are a very long time.

Here are some scripture references that give you assurance of God's purpose and ability.

1. *He who is the Glory of Israel does not lie or change his mind; for he is not a human being, that he should change his mind."* (1 Samuel 15:29)

God is not fickle like people who base their loyalty on circumstances. He says He will forgive when we repent. He does not say, "This is the twentieth time you have come. I'm not going to forgive you anymore." Nor does he say, "I pulled you out of trouble three times already. No more!" Our problem is not to take advantage of his mercy. He may not pull you out of trouble the fourth time the same way He did the first three. He may let you go through some trials to help you learn to make the right choices, but He does not change his mind about loving you or saving you.

2. *I establish my covenant with you: Never again will all life be destroyed by the waters of a flood; never again will there be a flood to destroy the earth."* (Genesis 12:1)

This is the promise he made to Noah that applies to you too. Never again will He destroy all life on earth in one catastrophe. That's you he is talking about. His desire is to save all life on earth. That is what Jesus Christ came to do.

3. *When tempted, no one should say, "God is tempting me." For God cannot be tempted by evil, nor does he tempt anyone.* (James 1:13)

God will not lie to you or deceive you. That is the tactic of the Devil. God will not pull you into sin away from Himself. He will always try to woo you to Himself because He loves you and wants the best for you. If the devil tempts you into sin, don't believe it is God. God will not tempt or goad you into doing evil deeds. Sometimes you might make a wrong choice that leads to something sinful. Know that God is ready to forgive when you repent.

4. *Be strong and courageous. Do not be afraid or terrified because of them, for the Lord your God goes with you; he will never leave you nor forsake you."* (Deuteronomy 31:6)

He will not leave you or forsake you. This means he will not take you down a path and leave you to fend for yourself or push you off a cliff. Even if other people abandon you, God will always be there. You can count on it. Don't rely on whether you see it or feel it. Count on it by faith.

5. *See, I set before you today life and prosperity, death and destruction. ^{16} For I command you today to love the Lord your God, to walk in obedience to him, and to keep his commands, decrees and laws; then you will live and increase, and the Lord your God will bless you in the land you are entering to possess.* (Deuteronomy 30:19)

This promise has conditions to it. If you fulfill the conditions, you can count on the fulfillment of the promise.

6. *But if serving the Lord seems undesirable to you, then choose for yourselves this day whom you will serve.* (Joshua 24:15)

God will not force you to choose Him even if He knows what is best for you. He may guide you, show you the way, and even encourage you to move with Him. God will honor your choice even when it is to move away from him. If you find yourself lost, and if you choose to repent and return back to him. He will still be there for you, waiting for you to step into his love.

Although God is all-powerful and all-knowing, He is not a despot. He gave you the gift of free will so that He can be in a loving relationship with you.

He loves you whether you like it or not.

You cannot change that. He gave Jesus Christ for your Salvation. He didn't ask you first. He didn't make you jump hoops first. Salvation was freely given, and He will not take it back. Now you have the chance to love him. When you accept this gift of Jesus as your Savior, you have made a choice to love the Father.

Discipline vs. Punishment

No discipline seems pleasant at the time, but painful. Later on, however, it produces a harvest of righteousness and peace for those who have been trained by it.

(Hebrews 12:11)

Discipline is *not* punishment. Punishment is a penalty imposed for a crime, offense, or violation. The penalty usually includes pain, loss, or retribution. The Lord gives many chances to repent and make a correction. Only when people refuse to come into alignment does God allow judgment to fall and punishment is mete out. Punishment is usually not a surprise. It is a written consequence and the offender can know the consequences before they commit the crime. If you park in a loading zone, you will be ticketed and must pay a fine. If you plan to murder someone, there are laws for pre-meditated murder.

Disciplines are put in place to give you freedom, not hem you in as some misunderstand. When someone is being corrected to come into order, it may be uncomfortable, feeling like punishment, but it is not.

Every January, many start thinking of New Year resolutions. Resolutions are only as good as the changes they produce. Discipline produces results. If you are disciplined in handling your money, you will not be caught with unpaid bills, or a poor credit rating. If you are disciplined in getting to work on time and work as you should, you reduce the chances of being fired. Disciplines do not pander to what you like to do. They order what you need to do to keep your life orderly and productive.

Pay attention to disciplines. Spiritual disciplines are more difficult to tackle than natural ones. Brush your teeth, shower, and wash your clothes are among the more obvious natural disciplines. Exercise, eat healthily, and refrain from smoking are sometimes more easily slacked on. Spiritual disciples are equally important, but too often, they slip by the wayside.

Here is a survey on how disciplined you are in your mind and heart. Be honest with yourself so you can improve. Rate yourself on a scale of 1-5. (1=never, 2=sometimes, 3 usually, 4=very often, 5=always.

_____**Work**: Do you make an effort to accomplish what is before you?
"Whatever you do, work at it with all your heart, as working for the Lord, not for human masters." (Colossians 3:23)

_____**Rest**: Do you allow your body and mind to rest?
"Remember the Sabbath day by keeping it holy." (Exodus 20:8)

_____**Giving**: Do you consistently give into the Kingdom of God? There are rewards when you give into the Kingdom. Do you give into the kingdom something besides money—time, skill, and help.
"Bring the whole tithe into the storehouse, that there may be food in my house. Test me in this," says the Lord Almighty, *"and see if I will not throw open the floodgates of heaven and pour out so much blessing that there will not be room enough to store it."* (Malachi 3:10)

_____**Corporate prayer**: Church, small group, prayer group

_____**Private prayer**: For other people, situations, and the nation

_____**Meditation**: Do you seriously meditate on the Word of God?
"Meditate on it day and night, so that you may be careful to do everything written in it. Then you will be prosperous and successful." (Joshua 1:8)

Divine Partnership   149

_____ **Fasting**: Do you fast to bring your body in submission to your spirit?

_____ Do you **fast** things other than food to get closer to God? (negative talk, TV, favorite pastime) (See Chapter 3, The Blessing Thief, page 71)

_____ **Warfare**: Do you war in the spirit for what you know is promised by God? (see Chapter on the Salvation Thief)

_____ **Worship**: Do you focus on the Lord *throughout your day?*

If you scored 50 points, you are excellent in spiritual discipline. 25 points is maintenance. Below 25, better start stepping up.

Responsibilities of daily life vie for your attention and time. If you are careful to engage in these things listed above, your life in the natural will be enriched. Your daily life will be in partnership with the Kingdom of God, lifting you above the world's demands.

You Wouldn't so You Couldn't.

Even after Jesus had performed so many signs in their presence, they still would not believe in him.

(John 12:37)

What blinds our eyes and hardens our hearts? Disobedience.

Obedience is a matter of will, not emotions or reason. Jesus says they "wouldn't, so they couldn't." Will comes before ability in the scheme of things.

"Wouldn't" addresses your choices and will. "Couldn't" address your ability. The will comes first. If you are not able to study, you need to check out your true desire to study. If you cannot keep appointments on time, you need to ask yourself, "Do I *really want* to be on time?" In my own experience, if I chose not to do my homework, then no matter how hard I tried, I could not do it. If I do choose not to be on time, then I will always be late.

Isaiah says, "They chose not to hear and repent or I would have healed them."

John 12:37, "But despite all the miracles he had done, most of the people *would not* believe he was the Messiah."

What are you choosing today? Are you choosing to do things God's way? If you are, you *could* do what's required, and He will be there to see you through.

For at least 12 years now, I am a Crossfit exerciser. Twelve years ago, at age 65, the Lord told me I needed to engage in serious exercise to stay fit for the work in His kingdom He had planned for me. I first started at the local gym, exercising my way at my own pace. I will admit it was by rote without challenge. I noticed I was not improving in strength, endurance, or mobility. My son then introduced me to Crossfit. I *chose* to join Crossfit, where a coach would teach me and encourage me. I chose to let a coach push me to do things I didn't think I could do. I am now stronger, and more fit than ever, doing exercises I thought would be impossible for me. I don't always *feel* like going to the gym, but I choose to, and that has made all the difference to me.

The pay-off is I can now lift my suitcase off the luggage carousel. I can run to catch a plane if I need to. I can walk through the Houston airport without being out of breath. I have the stamina to do 2-3 hour prayer meetings. At age 75, I went on a hike through the Amazon rainforest and walked through the city of Lima, Peru. I climbed the steps to Christ of the Andes statue in Brazil.

You'll amaze yourself once you choose to obey.

Tithes and Taxes

> "Bring the whole tithe into the storehouse, that there may be food in my house. Test me in this," says the Lord Almighty, "and see if I will not throw open the floodgates of heaven and pour out so much blessing that there will not be room enough to store it." (Malachi 3:8-10)

Today, the currency used to **pay** our taxes and **give** tithes is the same. In Jesus' day, the coinage for Roman taxes was minted by the Roman government. The temple tax was paid in temple coinage. *Paying* taxes and giving tithes initiate two different laws of money.

Civil taxes are computed according to a formula established by the government under which you live and are beneficiaries of its services—roads, sewage, water, electricity, bridges, storm drains, etc. In a democracy, the governing bodies of a country determine the taxes or at least approve them. If the citizens do not pay the assessed taxes, they will face financial penalties or even jail terms. Income taxes, property taxes, employer taxes, and sales taxes are the usual ones included. Once the government spends the money, it will need more to keep the machinery of government moving. If the government spends all its funds, it is bankrupt.

The tithe is more than a voluntary investment in the Kingdom of God. It is a faith choice that has a promise. Tithes are God's formula for you to give 10% of your gross income into his house for the work of the Kingdom. On the practical side, you are a beneficiary of this work in your church of pastoral care, education, child care, and the like. The Lord is realistic about the cost of operating a church. He never said, "You don't have to give any money to the church." Unless we contribute to the work of the church as seed money, its mission cannot be accomplished. It has been erroneously taught that we only need bring praise into His house. Because the church is "in" the world, it must pay the salaries of pastors, janitors, secretaries, bookkeepers, musicians, and those who provide "free services." The local church must also pay the electricity, water, heating, communications, and grounds maintenance bills. If there are no funds to support the expenses of the organization, it will go bankrupt.

Giving tithes is a membership investment in the Kingdom of God. Almost any organization has membership dues as a sign that you subscribe to their mission and actively participate in some way. It can be Girl Scouts, a golf club membership, or the Lions Club. If you do not pay the dues, you are just an observer and not a member. If you pay the dues but do not participate, you are an inactive member. There are many of both kinds in the church. The Lord calls us to be active, contributing members of His Kingdom.

God calls us to give tithes and offerings. When you bring in the tithe, the Lord will pour into you more than you gave. You will be able to give more and continue to increase. If you choose not to tithe, you are not fined or penalized. But, you will stop the promised blessings that are connected to giving. Lightning will not strike you if you do not give. Your capacity for gratitude and generosity increases when you tithe. A grateful heart can pull you out of your pity parties. So, be grateful you got up today, that you have food to eat, books to read, and a job. Too many times, we take things for granted so that we fail to see the blessings around us.

Paying taxes is a civic duty to support the lifestyle of the civil community. Paying taxes is required. It is not a choice. *Giving* tithes into God's house is a disciplined choice that will set in motion the law of multiplication. If you give tithes and offerings, you can expect abundance to flow to you from unknown sources.

> *The land produced vegetation: plants bearing seed according to their kinds and trees bearing fruit with seed in it according to their kinds. And God saw that it was good.* (Genesis 1:12)

Testimony by Eve

I left the dental office after my "no charge" X-ray and preliminary exam and now was faced with a possible $9,000 dental expense. I had been putting off this dental work for a long time, avoiding this huge expense. I just adjusted to the pain of an abscess and a broken tooth by chewing only on one side

Gary Keesee taught "Fixing the Money Thing" by sowing a financial seed with a name on it. I determined to test his instruction. I sowed a large seed into the Kingdom with the name "Dental Provision." The first dental office found a "mistake" on their bill for additional dental work, which reduced it from $460 to $155.

In the waiting room of the second dental specialist for my "no fee consult only" appointment, I saw an invitation to make a $100 donation to a clean water project in Africa. I agreed to the exam recommendation of a root canal and a crown for $1,192, with $100 of it going to the Africa clean water project. I was immediately ushered in for immediate attention. Same-hour appointments are unheard of, and, I didn't have to wait up to six weeks for it.

All this happened over six months going from one dentist to another, with appointments weeks apart, enduring the discomfort of a root canal, extraction, bone transplant, and abscess removal. I prayed over my seed. I learned how to navigate dental insurance. I was obedient in following the doctor's orders to regain my health and strength.

My Heavenly Father came through for me on my "Dental Provision" faith seed. He didn't give me a $9,000 check, but He reduced the overall cost drastically. The total expense went from $9,000 to $2,312. Put a name on your seed offering when you plant it.

Four Pitfalls to Avoid

We must never forget...(1 Corinthians 10:1-13)

There are three main ways you can gain wisdom. The first is through education. The second is through your own experience. The third is through others' experiences. Paul warns after being freed from your "Egypt" or slavery to sin, you need to be careful to avoid the pitfalls the Israelites faced.

1. **No idolatry.** God will not put up with idolatry. Although he is patient in drawing you to himself and keeping you focused on him, there will come a point where you lose contact with him if you keep making choices for other gods. Other gods offer spiritual paths that involve gods other than the Christian Godhead—Buddhism, Islam, Hinduism, voodoo, New Age, etc. He will give you *many* opportunities to return to Him by his grace, his mercy, and redemption. However, if you insist on choosing otherwise, He will not force you to accept Him. You will be left to your own devices.

2. **No sexual immorality.** Sexual immorality violates the sacredness of the physical body that was created to glorify God. If the body is defiled through sexual immorality, not only is it defiled, but future generations produced will be defiled. Yes, there is redemption. However, redemption is for getting you back on track, not as a license for continual sin. Sexual immorality is a wide door for Satan to enter and control your life.

3. **No testing the Lord.** Children test their parents. If told not to touch the vase, the child might touch it just to see what will happen if he does. If a child is told he will lose a privilege due to disobedience, he might disobey just to see if his parents will carry out the consequence. We are warned NOT to test the

Lord. Obey his Word without testing it. If He says He will fulfill a promise, believe Him. Do not manufacture situations to test God's hand. God acts according to **His** will, not yours.

4. **No grumbling.** What good does grumbling do? It magnifies the problem, makes you grumpy, and sets in negative thoughts. Grumbling focuses on the problem rather than the solution. When you grumble, you often make something that is not a problem into a problem and tangle up God's plan. Don't grumble about the weather. Life is still going to go on. Don't grumble about other people. They are still going to live their own lives as you must go on with your own. Don't grumble about your situation, as God has a plan that works.

If you have indulged yourself in any of these pitfalls, repent today and get back on track.

Don't Get Caught In Obsolescence

"From now on I will tell you of new things, of hidden things unknown to you." (Isaiah 48:6)

In October of 2007, I spent three weeks as a Global Volunteer in Xian, China bringing native English speaking to a school in Xianyang, about a one-hour drive from Xian. October 2014, I returned to China as a tourist, stopping in Xian again to visit my friends from 2007. I was saddened to learn that the thriving school of 2,000 students where we engaged students in English conversation was now closed. The city was originally built to accommodate the thousands of employees of Rainbow Company. Besides schools, there were daycares, hospitals, restaurants, shops, community centers, parks, and city infrastructure. Xianyang was the headquarters of the Rainbow Company, which made picture tube televisions back in 2007. With the advent of flat-screen televisions, this company's product became obsolete, and they were unable to retool and produce a modern appliance. Unfortunately, the company had to close all of its operations, which employed thousands. The city has shrunk in size and is now a place for the elderly and their grandchildren whose parents had to move away to find other work.

It's been seven years, and I wonder where those young people we encountered are today? Are they the ones on the streets of cities with a cell phone in hand, at computers surfing the internet, or sitting in the college classrooms? Oh, how I hope they have a bright future.

When things change quickly, and you do not adapt, you can be left behind doing things the old way. When the Holy Spirit moves into a new season, you need to move with Him. There are more complete understandings of the Word, new ways to pray, new ways to worship, and even new ways to "do church." Stay current with the move of God in His Kingdom.

Obedience Training

He replied, "Blessed rather are those who hear the word of God and obey it." (Luke 11:28)

Chelsea is our 4-year-old, 15-pound rescue Schnoodle puppy—schnauzer/poodle mix. She was a cute messy ball of fur, but after grooming, she was a cute, energetic dog. She quickly learned we were her friends. We fed, petted, played, and groomed her.

She was not friendly to other people, much less other dogs. So, on Saturday mornings for six weeks, we took her to dog obedience classes at the local park. There were about 15 other dogs of all ages and breeds in the class. Our Chelsea did not like other dogs around her. She would yelp, pull on the leash, and try to attack the biggest dogs with her 15-pound frame. Over the weeks, she learned "heel, sit, stay, and come" while on the leash. We could see she was restless in the company of other dogs. She could not be calm. The six-week classes gave us the rudiments of training but were by no means final.

In the weeks following, I tried the training methods we learned off-leash indoors using treats. I taught her to dance on her hind legs, catch treats, lie down, and play dead. This was all without a leash. The most difficult command was "stay." As soon as I put a treat down, she would jump for it. She eventually learned not to jump for it, but wait, though only for a few seconds. It's been a few months working on this obedience command. Now she will stay in the down position until I instruct her to "get it." Then she leaps forward toward the treat. She is so excited to get the treat she can hardly contain herself. Why is it so hard for her to "stay?"

Likewise, The Lord teaches us to obey his commands while on an invisible leash. We must be able to obey Him around people while under His command. The leash is really for our safety. I think when we are learning to be obedient to God, the most difficult command is "stay," because we want action. We want to do something. Sometimes we will make up something to do and say it's God. I have learned from my dog, Chelsea, that obedience training takes practice with more than a few trials.

Have you observed search and rescue dogs obey their master's voice commands or their hand signals while off-leash? Service dogs obey both the master and are alert to the dangers they are trained to observe. You could learn much about loyalty, obedience, and companionship from service dogs. Obey your Master's commands. Read on.

Peach Pie Gospel

The King will reply, 'Truly I tell you, whatever you did for one of the least of these brothers and sisters of mine, you did for me." (Matthew 25:40)

God will never ask you to do something that is simply impossible for you, but He will ask you to do something you can do. I don't think the Lord would ever ask me to move a piano by myself. If so, He will provide supernaturally. Since you can't know every plan of God, obey Him, and you will be a blessing as you are blessed.

God: Jenny, bake your best peach pie for your boss.

Jenny: That old grouch!! Why should I give him anything? All he does is complain. Nobody likes him. He goes around scowling at everybody.

God: (silence)

Jenny: He might think I'm fishing for a raise. That would not be good.

God: You know what I've asked you to do.

Jenny: I'll have to think about it. (She bakes the pie and the next morning gives it to her boss.)

Jenny: Morning, Mr. Copper (Grouch). I baked you a pie.

Mr. Copper: Did you think it was my birthday or something?

Jenny: No, but it can be if you want to make it so.

Mr. Copper: (Looking at the pie, tears begin to well up.)

Jenny: Is something wrong with the pie? You don't like peach?

Mr. Copper: I lost my wife a year ago and tomorrow is my birthday. I told God, "I wanted a piece of my wife's peach pie for my birthday." Of course, I knew that was impossible, but He brought me the peach pie through you.

Jenny: He loves you very much. He did the impossible for you.

Mr. Copper: I'll never doubt His love again.

Jenny: Happy Birthday!

God has so many ways for us to preach the gospel of love. Our obedience preaches louder than words from a pulpit. What is your pulpit? A peach pie? Transportation to the doctor? Being there to cheer someone on?

Peter was a fisherman. Jesus said to him, "Feed my sheep." Peter didn't say, "Wait a minute, I'm a fisherman. What do I know about sheep? I can't do that." Jesus said, "Follow me."

The Crown of Glory

And when the Chief Shepherd appears, you will receive the crown of glory that will never fade away. (1 Peter 5:4)

When St. Paul addresses the Corinthians on values, he points out that by human standards, wisdom, influence, and noble birth are highly regarded. College degrees, proficiency certificates, and educational accomplishments are only valuable when we use them. A greater market share, or the most political clout, and family position have advantages, but they do not necessarily guarantee success.

God, however, uses foolish things to outdo the wise. This is not logical thinking. Why would someone put their faith in something they cannot see or touch? God uses preaching, caring, and persuasion to draw people to himself. No army, organization, or monarchy heals the sick and sets captives free from sin. Only Jesus' disciples can do that. God uses people and things you least expect to show his glory—prostitutes, the poor, persecution, and even crucifixion.

What's God doing? What is he saying? God is turning our thinking to know that He values righteousness, holiness, and redemption. These are for all people of all races, heritage, and intellects. Only God can provide this through faith in Jesus Christ. No one can attain these on his own.

Faith precedes everything. Miracles *follow* those who have faith. Wisdom comes to those who stand in awe of God. Understanding *follows* obedience through faith.

When you walk into a dark room, I would tell you, "Touch the wall by the door and feel for a lever. Flip the lever upward." If you obeyed, the lights in the room would go on. Because of your obedience to the directions, you now have the wisdom that whenever you want light in that room, you need to flip the lever upward. You also understand that the lever is on the wall near the door. In the future, when you walk into a dark room, you will look for a light switch of some kind to turn on the lights. Although you may not know how electricity is wired through the walls to the lights or how it comes from the power plant, you know how to make it work.

When you stand in awe of God, you will hear His instructions. When you obey, you will see the results. You will be able to use the wisdom and understanding for future situations.

If you walk in righteousness, holiness, and obedience through faith in Jesus, you will be a wise person of understanding and influence. That is the crown of glory he desires for you.

One Step Ahead

*For he will command his angels concerning you
to guard you in all your ways.* (Psalm 91:11)

In January 2020, my husband and I had the opportunity to cruise the Amazon River on a Cunard cruise ship. The trip started from Fort Lauderdale, Florida, through the Caribbean Islands and into the mouth of the Amazon. It took two days to go up the Amazon to the confluence and two days back to the Atlantic Ocean. It was an amazing adventure seeing ancient cities, going on nature hikes, and floating on the Amazon River, the largest river in the world. Our trip continued on the eastern South American coast ending in Rio de Janeiro.

I had arranged for an independent city tour of Rio de Janeiro through Viator. Rich and I waited at the cruise port as instructed where our guide was to meet us. After waiting 45 minutes, I decided to call the tour company. I did not have international calling on my phone, so I looked around for help. I overheard some young people who seemed to be locals near me speaking a mix of Portuguese and English. Explaining I did not have access to international calling, I asked them to call the tour company for me. They were more than happy to help.

One fellow called and, fortunately, could speak in Portuguese to the tour office and explain my plight. After a couple of calls back and forth, I was told the tour was already in progress and they could not pick us up. We could find our own way to join them if we wanted or get our money back.

It's difficult being in a foreign country and not able to speak the language. A gal in the group suggested I get a taxi tour or an independent private tour. I told her I needed a guide that spoke good English as we had bad experiences with tour guides with strong foreign accents, and we could not understand what they were saying. We wanted to learn as much as we could about the city in addition to seeing the major sites.

She went to a group of tour operators and interviewed them for me. She then waved me over and suggested I hire Romero. He spoke good English, his price was fair, and this would be a private tour.

Romero led us three blocks away to a parking garage to his car. Was this déjà vu of our Xian, China car ride? We stood at the car park entrance, and he drove up to pick us up. We got in, and off we went.

Romero was an experienced and knowledgeable tour guide. He gave us the history of the city, the news, the neighborhoods, as well as the tourist sites we wanted to see. We soon realized he was well known in the tour guide industry as he managed to get us VIP passes to the head of the lines in all places. We had a wonderful day. He returned us to our ship on time.

What started as a disappointment turned out to be a wonderful day with the help of the locals who so graciously looked after us. I believe they were all angels.

While on the cruise, we heard the news of cruise ships stranded offshore because of COVID-19 outbreaks. Ships were not allowed to dock to let passengers disembark. There were no COVID-19 incidents that we knew about on our cruise ship.

We spent two extra days in Brazil, touring Rio, then headed home. We flew from Rio to Houston with an overnight stay before landing in Los Angeles. We arrived home in two days. Two days after we got home, all flights from Brazil were banned from the USA because of COVID-19 outbreaks in Brazil, especially in Rio de Janeiro.

We narrowly made it home before the shutdown.

The Lord's timing is impeccable. This was the last of our international traveling until restrictions are lifted.

EPILOGUE

Children of The King

Because I have personally experienced God's hand in my life, I am spurred on to write this book. I could not always see God's hand at work during certain situations, but I certainly could in hindsight.

The mature Christian holds the Word of God in the heart, body, and soul as well as the mind. Trust builds over the years. When you recognize God's faithfulness in little things, you will appreciate how He is there in a crisis. You will never cease to be amazed at how God always has a long view of things way beyond our understanding.

Trust and obey are the watchwords.

Some things are simple, and some are more challenging to your human instincts.

These stories are accounts of some experiences when God showed up in wonderful ways in my life. I hope you will be encouraged to look back in your life and discover how His hand was on you. Nothing was too small or too big. Also, anticipate he is not going to quit now. You are too precious.

Help in Time of Need

Let us then approach God's throne of grace with confidence, so that we may receive mercy and find grace to help us in our time of need. (Hebrews 4:16)

Since I am a very competent person, I dangerously thought I could do everything myself, and I must. When I could not do things for myself, I went without.

As a young mother with three children under the age of eight, I suffered a bout with bursitis in the shoulder. Because of excruciating pain, my husband took me to the emergency room at midnight. We took the three young children who waited in the emergency room lobby. The treatment consisted of a cortisone injection and some pills for the next week. I was to see the doctor the next day for a follow-up.

I took the medication as directed and, the next day, packed up my three children in the car and headed for the doctor. By the time I got there, I was very sick. It seems the dosage of the medication would have been fine for a 6 foot, 200-pound man, but I was all of 4'10" and 85 pounds, so I was suffering from an overdose. The doctor said all I could do now was to let the medication take its course and run through my body. Needless to say, I was very sick. As I drove home, I had to stop twice to vomit on the roadside. The children were very quiet, but I knew they were scared just watching me. Why didn't I think to ask someone to drive me and/or care for my children? I can do it myself!

After I returned home, I was racked with vomiting and could not attend to the children. Though they played nicely on their own, I realized this was not the way to leave them. I finally telephoned for help from a friend who came over immediately with her older daughter to care for the children. My friend cleaned me up and put me to bed. Her daughter cared for the children as she then went home only to return with dinner for the family. By the time my husband came home, all was under control. This friend also checked on me for the next few days and provided dinners for us.

From this event, I learned my **self-sufficiency was pride**. The Lord had to let me go down to utter helplessness before I would come to my senses and call for help. Had it not been for my concern for the children, I probably would have "toughed it out." The Lord will send angels in the form of others to help you in the time of need if we would but ask.

Accept help. You will be blessed.

God Plans the Future

*Dear friends, since God so loved us,
we also ought to love one another.*

(1 John 4:11)

Our adventure in China led to the changed lives of a Chinese family in a way we never imagined. We should never underestimate how the Lord uses us to change the course of people's lives. God knows what we don't know. By following his direction, we see wonders.

In 2007, my husband and I went to a city in China for three weeks as Global Volunteers to teach conversational English at a village school. We traveled an hour and a half to the school daily, accompanied by an English-speaking guide who served as translator and interpreter. She was a teacher quite knowledgeable of the customs and ways of the city. The daily ride gave us plenty of time to talk and get acquainted. We shared stories of our life in the USA, and she about life in China, the customs, and the traditions.

We were free to explore on our own on the weekends, but our guide insisted that she and her husband take us around. Of course, we accepted. Not being able to communicate in Chinese would make us vulnerable to all sorts of misadventures. We experienced museums, restaurants, and shops we would have never found or navigated on our own. We got to know them better and met their young son briefly. They made our time so special.

After our three-week stay, we invited them to the USA to visit us in California. She said it was only a dream of hers and doubted she would ever be able to go. We said this was an open invitation for any time in the future.

Epilogue

Less than a year later, I received an email from our interpreter. "We are coming to the USA. We want to stay with you. My husband, son, and I are coming."

"Yes!" Fortunately, we have a large home to accommodate guests.

In the next email from her, she wrote, "My sister is coming too. Our other son is coming from Arizona to meet us. Is that ok?"

"Of course. How long will they be staying? "

"Six weeks."

She was in a quandary about activities for her twelve-year-old son. He was "just a kid" and probably would not like to hang out with adults. His English is not very good, and maybe he could stay home and do his studies which he will bring along.

I thought, "Why would a 12-year-old boy come from China to do homework?" The Youth Leaders at my church agreed to shepherd him at the Youth Camp that week. Although he had minimal English, they welcomed him with open arms.

I collected camping gear such as a tent, sleeping bag, and toiletries that he would need, plus got some "camping clothing" from the local thrift shop. I packed him up as I had my children. The family arrived at the airport at 10 p.m. on a Sunday and at 7:30 a.m. the next day, I dropped him off at the church. He was nervous but adventurous. The youth leaders were very welcoming, and off they went for the next five days. The youth leaders were trustworthy, so we had no worries.

After five days of youth camp, we found him beaming with joy. He had made friends, picked up English teenage slang phrases, and met Jesus. He was only too anxious to get his mother and father, brother & aunt into church the next Sunday. When the group gave a "camp presentation" at church, he was right in there with them. His older brother, having been in college in the USA, had heard about church and Jesus, but now, after seeing his younger brother beaming, was convinced that being a Christian was a good thing.

During their stay, we went to shopping malls, looked at new American cars, and visited model homes. On the food scene, we introduced them to American restaurants and the diverse offerings of international cuisines here in California. I taught their young son how to make sandwiches, cook instant noodles, and cook eggs. I showed the ladies how to use a dishwasher, washing machine, and various kitchen appliances. Her husband, who was fearful of starving in America, came to love Souplantation and breakfast buffets. They even squeezed in a trip to Las Vegas, the Grand Canyon, and a short tour to New York City. It was a whirlwind trip.

This Chinese family's trip to our home changed their lives in ways none of us could have predicted. A dream of ever traveling to the USA turned into a world paradigm shift.

Meanwhile, the young man who went to church camp said he wanted to attend high school as an American teenager. He studied to improve his English language skills and passed the required exams to be accepted to a private Catholic school as a freshman. He was "adopted" by a loving family and had "brothers and a sister" in his new family. With China's one-child policy, he never had a sibling to grow up with. An American family with brothers and a sister was beyond his wildest dreams. This was a real joy to him. He graduated near the top of his class while participating in sports and science competitions.

His mom was able to visit him during those 5 years. He was accepted to the University of Wisconsin, where he graduated with a Bachelor of Science in engineering and was accepted to the graduate school. Before completing graduate school, he secured an internship with an engineering company. On occasional visits to California, he would connect with us. We watched him grow into a fine young man.

A Bout With Malaria

"For I know the plans I have for you," declares the Lord, "plans to prosper you and not to harm you, plans to give you hope and a future." (Jeremiah 29:11)

What moved the Peace Corp officials to send our son home early, no matter how much he begged to finish his commitment? No matter what they called it, **I believe it was the Holy Spirit and the Hand of God.**

This was February. "Mom, I'm coming home early," was the news from our oldest son Charles, making a long-distance call from Zambia. These were days when long-distance calls were rare and very expensive. He was serving in the US Peace Corps, and his two-year commitment would be up in August. He was disappointed and in tears. He wanted to complete his commitment, but the Peace Corp directors told him they were sending him home because he was depressed.

After being discharged and before leaving Africa, he decided to spend a week backpacking in Namibia and then come home by way of Germany. He said he might as well see as much as possible while he was on the African continent, not knowing when or if he would ever return.

We welcomed him home after his long trip from Africa through Germany to Los Angeles. At the airport, he looked very thin, scruffy, and though sad to leave Zambia, happy to be home with us.

Within a week, he said he wasn't feeling well, maybe a cold. He thought all the traveling made him susceptible to colds. I gave him the usual cold remedies, and he slept a lot. After a week, his fever spiked, and he suspected it was malaria. He said he had seen this in other PCV (Peace Corps Volunteers) while in Zambia. First, we used cold packs on his face to bring down the fever. When that wasn't enough, he took cold showers. The fever would spike, then go down in a couple of hours, and things would be normal. Forty-eight hours later, the fever would return and spike a bit higher, then subside.

After a week of this routine, I took him to the hospital emergency room one evening at about 8 PM. The local emergency room did not rush him through because he was coherent and seemed to be normal. Nothing looked like an emergency. A doctor finally saw him, and by then, things were "normal." He told the doctor he had just returned from Africa and suspected this was malaria. This doctor was unfamiliar with malaria and gave him a referral to an infectious disease doctor.

The referred infectious disease doctor could not see him until next week. We were in for another week of spiked fever.

The next day the spiked fever hit again. Charles was shaking and shivering, and his fever was very high. He begged me to fill the tub with cold water and ice so he could get in and get some relief.

Several months before, the stopper in our bathtub broke, and I didn't get around to fixing it since we always used the shower and seldom used the stopper in the bathtub. There was no way our bathtub would fill with water. I then called a friend who lived five minutes away to ask if we could use his bathtub.

"Of course," he said, "come right over. What crazy thing are you folks doing now?"

"I'll tell you when we get there. By the way, collect all the ice you can and fill the tub with cold water!"

When we got there, he ushered us into the bathroom, where Charles got into the tub. The ice he had was not enough, so he ran next door to his neighbor for more.

"Nancy, I need all your ice!

"Sure. What's going on?"

"Charles needs an ice bath to counteract the fever."

Nancy, a nurse at Hoag Hospital, was more than curious about the story.

She said, "Take him to Hoag Hospital immediately, and I will call

Dr. Hudson, the infectious disease doctor there. I know him personally and will ask him to get the ER to admit Charles."

We bundled the shaking, freezing, fevering young man and hustled him to the ER at Hoag Hospital. When we arrived, the fever had dropped, and he seemed normal. Because of the alert, ER admitted him immediately and began the admitting process.

We waited a long time in the admitting room until the attending doctor arrived, saying he got the call from the infectious disease doctor with instructions. After some research, Dr. Hudson's instructions came.

Our son was admitted and began treatment at the hospital. We learned that Dr. Hudson had studied malaria in Africa, and when he learned our son was in Zambia, he knew immediately how to treat this strain of malaria. After a week of hospitalization with IVs and careful monitoring, Charles was ready to return home with additional meds.

We were told that he had a serious case of malaria and that if he had not come home when he did, he could have easily died in Zambia since this treatment is not readily available there. Our son was living in the bush, on the outskirts of any major city, and it would have been nearly impossible to get him medical help. He is now malaria-free and can only be re-infected by a malaria-carrying mosquito.

As I looked back, I saw how the Lord knows the end from the beginning. He knows things we don't are coming, and he plans for our good. Had I fixed the tub stopper, we would not have gone to our neighbors, who would not have gone to his nurse neighbor, who would not have contacted the right doctor immediately.

We also learned later that there was tribal fighting in the Congo at that time. Our son's village was two miles from the Congo border, and months later, the fighting spilled into his village area. That area was so remote that not much was paid attention to it. Tribal fighting does not respect country borders.

Before, Beside, Behind

You hem me in behind and before, and you lay your hand upon me. Such knowledge is too wonderful for me, too lofty for me to attain. (Psalm 139:5)

In times of **sudden events**, when you don't know what is going to happen, you can stand on your faith, knowing He goes before you, beside you, and behind you always.

While touring Cambodia in 2007, my husband and I were in a serious auto accident. The driver was going too fast on a one-and-a-half-lane remote dirt road when he lost control of the SUV. It rolled over twice, landing in a dry rice field. My husband had his head down as he was feeling car sick. I was seated in the middle of the back seat, holding between my knees, a green coconut with a straw in it. It was for Rich's car sickness. Riding with us was our son Charles to my left and Ron in the front passenger seat. I was somewhat in a daze when I heard Charles yell, "Slow down!" Before I knew it, we were thrown and rolling in the car that rested on the right side. The only persons who had seatbelts were Charles and Ron.

Once the car rested, Charles climbed out the window, and Ron climbed through the broken windshield. Rich and I were lying on our sides inside the vehicle. The people from the next car of our caravan thought they were going to help strangers. They pulled us out through the sunroof.

My husband and I suffered vertebrae injuries. Our son walked away shaken and bruised. Ron suffered cuts and bruises, and the driver fled the scene. Two fellows of our group were doctors who attended to us immediately. I believe that was God's provision as one of the doctors was going to cancel coming, but his wife urged him to go without her.

He formerly was a Peace Corps volunteer who practiced emergency aid in primitive conditions. In this remote area, there is no 911 call to rely on. The group reorganized, and one car took us back to the clinic in Siem Reap. I was lying on the back seat of an SUV for the two-hour ride to the nearest hospital. Dr. KG accompanied us, Charles and Ron, on the ride back. After an hour, I felt pain in the bouncing of the car. The driver stopped so Dr. KG, and Charles could make a back splint for me of sticks gathered from the side of the road and a ripped T-shirt. Rich and Ron were doing ok. We continued the final hour to the clinic.

The clinic was rather ill-equipped in both staff and facilities. Fortunately, we had our own doctor to attend to us. I remember Dr. KG giving me a shot for pain which was heavenly. When our daughter-in-law arrived, she swatted mosquitoes and flies with a bug zapper. The clinic moved Rich and me into separate treatment rooms until I told them we were husband and wife. Our son sent an email to notify our daughter and alert our friends to pray. He also contacted the trip insurance company about the accident so they would cover the expenses.

Within 24 hours, we were flown to Bangkok Bumrungrad Hospital, Thailand. There the X-rays and scans showed we did not need surgery of any kind, just bed rest and care in movement. A Swiss doctor who spoke good English attended us. I had a neck brace that immobilized me. I could hardly move. I needed assistance for everything, even in showering.

While spending eleven painful days in the Thailand hospital, I could have moaned, "Why did this happen to us?" or "Praise the Lord, I got into an accident!" I did neither.

I said, "I can't wait to see how You are going to get us out of this pickle." I stood on my faith, knowing God was pulling us through. We were in the best hospital in Southeast Asia.

I believe the Holy Spirit prompted me to purchase travel insurance for the first time. I was looking for the cancellation option, but He knew I would need more. The insurance paid all the medical costs, including the airlift to Thailand and business class air back to the US. The Thai doctor advised, "Lay on your back as much as possible for the next 100 days, then you will be fine." Once home, I lay on my back for 100 days and recovered fully.

We Are Alive!

For he will command his angels concerning you to guard you in all your ways. (Psalm 91:11)

The pain didn't abate, but neither did the laughing.

After being rescued from a single-engine plane crash on our Zambian trip in 2000, we were rescued from the jungle and brought to safety in the Kasanka National Park.

The four Vogls (Rich, Marcia, Charles, James), Pilot Robert, and the German doctor would go on with Edmond, the park ranger, to Kasanka National Park Camp for the night.

Before leaving the site of the rescue plane, the doctor said to me, "How is the pain?" He was asking about my foot which was crushed when the seat collapsed in the crash.

"I really don't feel any pain."

"If you would like, I could give you a shot of pain killer to deaden the pain. Would you like that?"

"I think I will do fine. Motrin will be enough."

"Here's some Motrin to tide you over," he said as he put his medicine bag on the parked plane.

We rode for two hours at 60 mph on the dark Zambian road. Because of construction, this road was down to one lane in places with headlights coming straight on. Fortunately, there was very little traffic, and the careful driver avoided any crashes. We started at 7 p.m. on a paved road for the first hour and a half. The last 45 minutes were on a bumpy trail road through the forest. It was like the earlier ride, but this time in the dark.

Edmond radioed ahead for the cooks to make a hot meal and prepare six beds.

We arrived at the Kasanka National Park, where a hot spaghetti meal was waiting for us.

"Come sit down at the campfire," was the invitation as they served us punch. "The meal will be ready in a moment."

We were escorted to picnic tables under an awning and served a delicious meal. It was sure good as we were starved and tired. The staff at the park had prepared the individual cabins, which were spread over the circular campground. Each cabin accommodated two people, and the toilets were outhouses separate from the cabins.

"Mom, can you walk to your cabin?" James asked. "We can carry you."

"Let me help," Robert said as he rushed over. The two locked arms, forming a "chair" for me to sit on so they could carry me across the field.

We were all assigned and retired for the night. Rich and I settled in for the night.

"Oooooow," I wailed. The pain in my foot was increasing. "I can't sleep!" I said as I rolled side to side on the bed." It was about 2 a.m.

"I'll get the Motrin. Where is it?" asked Rich as he rummaged around through our things.

"Do we have water?" I asked.

"No."

"How am I going to take the pill?"

"Can't you just swallow it?"

"Ooooow," I cried with tears streaming down my face. The Motrin wasn't helping much.

About an hour later, "Rich, I have to go to the bathroom!"

"Can you walk? How about hobble?"

"I'll try, but it's not easy." I hobbled to the door of the cabin. Once outside, we had a plan.

"I don't think I can carry you, but I'll hold you up," Rich said as he put his arm under my armpits to brace me. We only got 10 feet out.

"Maybe I should carry you on my back like a kid?" as he bent down so I could climb on.

As I leaned over to put my arms around his neck, "Ha-ha-ha, hee, hee-hee," I started to giggle. Then Rich started to giggle. Before we knew it, we were both on the ground laughing uncontrollably until our sides ached.

We were laughing under the clear African sky. The stars were shining over us. WE ARE ALIVE! WE ARE ALIVE!!! The tension of the day finally lifted, and we were filled with silliness laughing hysterically. The bright moon lit up the campus. The crickets were chirping. The cool night breeze was wafting over us. We felt such joy.

Eventually, I crawled to the outhouse and back with Rich at my side, also giggling and laughing. We lay on the bunks trying to sleep, but I would start giggling, and we would start all over again. The pain didn't abate, but neither did the laughing.

We didn't get much sleep laughing until 5 a.m.

Saying Goodbye

Your sun will never set again, and your moon will wane no more; the Lord will be your everlasting light, and your days of sorrow will end. (Isaiah 60:20)

Be gracious, and kindly let them go.

Dad was 93 years old and getting very tired. He had little energy to eat or do his favorite word puzzles or jigsaw puzzles. He slept most of the time in his favorite chair. He was not in pain, nor was he sick, just old. The doctor said his body was just wearing out.

In August of 2010, the whole family gathered in Hawaii for our son's wedding. I knew in my spirit seeing his oldest grandson marry would be Dad's last big celebration. We did everything possible to get him to the wedding. He mustered all his energy for this event which was joyful and splendid.

I also knew in my spirit that it was time for me to say goodbye to him. Because there was so much family activity, there was hardly any opportunity for a discrete visit alone. I had a chance to be with him fortuitously orchestrated by the Lord. When I asked if he was afraid to die, he said, "No. When the good Lord says it is my time, I will go." Dad said he was tired, and his body was just worn out.

I got close to him, as he could not hear well. I told him I loved him very much. He was my hero through the years. He just smiled. Then I said, "This may be the last time I see you this side of heaven, so I want to say goodbye. It's okay to go when the Lord calls. Mom will be fine, and we will look after her. You provided for her well through the years, and there is enough for the rest of her days." He just said, "Ok." Then I prayed for him, thanking the Lord for having him for my Dad and asking the Lord to gently lead him home.

Dad's last piece of business was to sell the family home. It had been two years since they moved to senior/assisted living. They would never move back. The sale would ensure mom's care. In December, the house was listed for sale, and it sold within a week. While under hospice care, he was surrounded by the most caring and loving attendants who guided him and Mom through the last days. No trauma, no drama, just gentle, loving care.

On January 4, 2011, my sister called, saying Dad had passed on quietly in his sleep with his beloved wife of 68 years at his side. I knew in my heart he was answering the Lord's call to go home, and my prayer for him had been answered.

Though difficult, I knew I was to say goodbye the previous August. Saying goodbye made me know life and death are in the Lord's hands. I'm glad I obeyed. If you have a loved one nearing the end of life, do not be afraid to say goodbye when the opportunity arises. It is not hurrying their passing. It is sending them on their way with a blessing. Be gracious, and kindly let them go.

Holy Spirit Travel Agent

We can make our plans, but the Lord determines our steps. (NLT*) (Proverbs 16:9)

My God is mindful of ALL things concerning me. These are quiet miracles that He so graciously bestowed during a time of releasing a parent.

My sister's usual phone greeting is "Hey, Mesash!" using my childhood nickname. This time I heard my sister say, "Marcia…" I knew this call was serious.

It was July 2013. Mom had a serious emergency room episode and was being admitted to hospice as her health was deteriorating. She had two prior open-heart surgeries, the last being at age 88. The doctors did not think she could survive a third one at age 93. She was not suffering nor was in pain, but her heart was giving out. Without hesitation, I decided I would go visit her in Honolulu as this might be my last chance while she lived.

Our daughter Stephanie said she would like to go along, taking her children (mom's great-grandchildren, ages 5 and 2) for the last visit. Summertime plane tickets to Hawaii were at their premium rate. While browsing the Website, I noticed the first-class seat required the same number of frequent flyer miles as the economy seat. Thinking there was some mistake, I called the airline to inquire.

"That's correct, ma'am. There are only four seats available in first class on that flight."

---

*Holy Bible, New Living Translation, copyright © 1996, 2004, 2015 by Tyndale House Foundation. Used by permission of Tyndale House Publishers, Inc., Carol Stream, Illinois 60188. All rights reserved

I quickly booked them with the click of the mouse. Four first-class seats for $5 each with frequent flyer miles was a gift from heaven.

The Hawaii Kai Senior Living, where my mother was staying, has guest apartments for visiting relatives. Six of us stayed for $120 a day, with all meals and parking included. This was cheaper than any local hotel!

It was a blessed few days as we were able to celebrate Mom's 93rd birthday with a quiet family-only lunch. She was surprised yet happy that we all flew in from California to see her. We were able to express love and say goodbye for the last time. It was bittersweet but joyful, giving us all closure. We were sad on the way back to the airport but knew in our hearts this was part of life.

Mom passed quietly on September 1. Again, I made travel arrangements to Hawaii on short notice. My husband and I would stay for two weeks until September 17 to take care of Mom's legal and personal business. I had a coupon that required a 30-day booking window for complimentary four nights in a hotel, expiring on September 17. I explained our situation to the agent and since we were going to Hawaii anyway, I would like the reservation to be effective immediately. The agent gave us our complimentary four-night hotel stay with immediate confirmation. Favor!

Again, flight tickets purchased under seven days are expensive. However, because this was in the middle of the Labor Day weekend, we were able to find discount fares. Besides, there were so many empty seats, we could spread out in comfort.

The car rental company had an option called "wild card"—$200 for 14 days—for a car of *their* choice. Upon arrival, the only available car was a red minivan. I reluctantly accepted the minivan because parking is difficult in Honolulu. Little did I know, we would need this minivan to move Mom's belongings out of her apartment. With this minivan, we completed the move in two days. Provision again!

Parking was always at a premium, but where ever we went, I found a convenient parking space that was ample for a minivan. Somehow, when I got where I needed to be, a parking space was waiting for me. Some would call it luck. I call it provision.

Our oldest son rerouted his travel from Thailand to California through Honolulu to be there for the funeral. Because this change was due to a death in the family, his trip insurance covered the $2,000 flight change fee. Another God provision.

In the past, Mom's clothes were too large for me. Her clothing, sizes that ranged from small to medium, now fit me. How could all those sizes fit me now? It's a miracle. I came away with a new wardrobe.

Abundant Life

"Help me be a grown-up Christian" was the request I heard from my clients through the years. With teachings and sharing my personal experiences, I have shown you steps for growing into Christian maturity, producing fruit, and bearing seeds for the next generation. A fruit tree does not strain or worry about what variety of fruit it will bear. It simply is itself. The surrounding ground and climate affect the quality and quantity of fruit. The tree does not work for its place, it does not pay for its favor, nor does it change its location unless the farmer moves it. So with you, no striving, no earning, and no self-transplanting is needed. The currency of heaven is obedience, praise, and worship. Do not let the world overcome you, have a spiritual strategy, and fulfill your heavenly destiny. Look for signs of how the guidelines I have shared can work in your life, bringing you joy and fulfilling your purpose.

Free download.
How to Forgive Anyone, Present or Absent.
www.MarciaChangVogl.com

About the Author

Marcia Chang Vogl is an ordained minister with graduate degrees in Education including a Doctorate in Practical Ministry, She serves as the Director of Bethany Projects with Hidden With Christ Ministries.

She creates and implements workshops for groups of five to fifty people concerning spiritual issues. As a minister, she has ministered to a Chinese-speaking church (with an interpreter), to a group of pastors, and to adult fellowships. She leads prayer meetings, seminars, and retreats (by invitation), in addition to private prayer counseling sessions regularly. Her focus is on inner healing and deliverance for all God's people.

Her combined experiences as a former public school teacher and a college mentor, give breadth and depth to her teaching. The leaders she has mentored have impacted the world in business, education, churches, and faith-based organizations throughout the US and internationally, including the nations of Asia and Africa. Her passion for traveling the world and serving as a Global Volunteer in Xian, China, and Hanoi, Vietnam has provided her with culturally relevant experiences which are expressed in her books.

Publications: (found on Amazon.com)
The Path Forward
Dancing with God, The Christian Journey to Live Supernaturally
Training to Reign, The Christian Guide to Spiritual Maturity.

Her articles and devotionals have been published in *Christiandevotions*.us online magazine, *Purpose Magazine*, a Menno Media publication, and *The Secret Place*, Judson Press.

Find out more about Marcia and her ministry at:
www.MarciaChangVogl.com
https://BethanyProjects.org

Ministry Scope

Bethany Projects is a Ministry for Men and Women offered through:

1. Published books: *The Path Forward, Dancing With God* and *Training to Reign with God* (Amazon.com)
2. Private prayer sessions: in person, and online
3. Mentoring groups, Retreats, and Workshops
4. Blogs, Devotionals, and Videos / Audio Recordings online
5. Social Media: website (MarciaChangVogl.com) Facebook/BethanyProjects, Instagram, and LinkedIn,

Mary and Martha Fellowship reaches to women who are a very important part of the Church and society. The fellowship offers:

1. Personal Prayer and Spiritual counseling to establish a Biblical mindset.
2. Godly fellowship and encouragement.
3. Training to walk with the Holy Spirit.
4. Mentoring for ministry in prayer, worship, and spiritual warfare.
5. Corporate worship.

Mentoring Meetings for men and women develop skills in practical Christian living. It is a mentored safe place to use the gifts of the spirit and explore Biblical tenants as they apply to daily life. Gatherings include corporate worship, Godly fellowship, and celebration.

For an invitation to join any group, or for a private prayer session submit your request by email to Marcia.Prayer@Gmail.com

Marcia brings to her ministry life experiences of international travel, multiple professional careers, a 50+ year marriage, and the rearing of an international family.

Free Downloads
How to Forgive Anyone Present or Absent
30 Day Family Reconciliation Devotional

www.MarciaChangVogl.com
www.DancingwithGodBook.com
www.TrainToReignbook.com
www.LinkedIn.MarciaChangVogl
https://BethanyProjects.org
Marcia.Prayer@Gmail.com

www.ingramcontent.com/pod-product-compliance
Lightning Source LLC
Chambersburg PA
CBHW071239070526
44583CB00017B/2247